MW01258599

World-Class Intercessors

Dawn of the Dread Champions

Judy Sullivan

Dedicated to the memory of
Tim Sullivan
Much loved husband, father, grandfather,
and my inspiration.

FIRST EDITION

Cover Design- Kandi Evans
Layout Design- Michael R. Carter

ISBN-13: 978-1515344360
ISBN-10: 1515344363

Printed in the United States of America
Set in 12pt. ITC Galliard

Contents

Part Three: Strategic-Level Intercession

Appendix:

Foreword

Judy Sullivan came into my life at one of my lowest points. The business we counted on to pay our son's medical bills was struggling, and the ongoing distractions had become disabling. Fallout was evident everywhere—unpaid bills at work and at home, with my marriage crumbling under the weight of it all.

Thankfully, our cries for help were answered the day Ashley, our former business partner, my husband, and I agreed we needed more than the prayers we prayed at our home church. We wandered into a conversation during our regular sales meeting that, looking back, was anything but random. "I heard a guy talking about professional intercessors the other day," said Ashley. "Maybe we should look into that."

We didn't have two dimes to rub together, and we were desperate. Surely God would provide for the direction our hearts were taking us. And He did. Our internet search quickly took us to Sozo Services where we met Judy, and in one accord, we knew we had found our match.

While we have never viewed the idea of combining our prayers with an intercessory team as a "formula," for us it proved to be the antidote to our problems. Strongholds that had plagued us for years began to come down. Bottlenecks of all sizes that most called "typical" of our industry were removed. Revenues soared despite a sagging economy. Supply chains opened up, current customers answered their phones, new customers opened their doors, personnel issues went away, and relationships breathed again.

Challenges continued, as they do and always will. But we now had a solid phalanx of protection, discernment, and encouragement—an unyielding protective covering led by humble, fierce prayer warriors storming heaven on our behalf.

This book is about much more than an intercessor who prays for businesses, but this is how we came to know Judy. Along our journey, she has become more than my intercessor. She has become my friend—a friend who has gone toe-to-toe with whatever stands against my marriage, my children, and my business, changing the face of my community and the state in which we live.

A few years after we began working with Judy, I attended a breakout session on the topic of intercession at a global economic summit. The speaker predicted that within our lifetimes it would become rare for kingdom-minded business owners to operate *without* an intercessory arm working on their behalf. Having personally experienced the "before and after" of this in our own business, I could easily understand why.

Is it any wonder that the forces of hell squarely align themselves against those who dare to traverse the mountains they are called to and pursue the summits they were born to occupy? Is it any wonder that another level of intercession would become a lethal weapon of choice, defying all worldly measures?

I still stand amazed at the changes that have taken place since we enlisted Judy and her team of professional intercessors. Some of the change occurred, no doubt, from simply being able to communicate with trusted listeners the "ins and outs" of business and our daily challenges during our weekly prayer call, or what we affectionately referred to as "The Call." Most of the changes took place following what was heard, seen, or discerned "between the lines" during our conversations. Then we prayed over, believed for, cut off, redirected, commanded, reversed, and received, all with thanksgiving. By faith, we believed for outcomes ahead of time and stood with those who were constantly standing in the gap for us. As a result, unreasonable favor followed us, and our business has flourished beyond our wildest imagination.

But all of us are so much more than the work of our hands. In her book, Judy boldly asserts, *"Imagine what can happen when the people you pray for start to see who they really are."* That's why "The Call" did not merely include topics of conversation crucial to the success of our business, because business owners are more than simply owners of businesses. Despite the fact that the enterprises we are building consume most of our waking hours, we are moms and dads, brothers and sisters, community members, friends and associates. We are philanthropists, inventors, activists, educators, the sculptors of society, the oil in the engines of the communities, states, and countries in which we live.

Which of these roles could not benefit from the strength provided through consistent intercession? What part of any journey is not multiplied through the depth of the channel created by world-class vessels of intercession?

Indeed, I believe it is because our Founding Fathers held fast to the power of prayer that we are and remain, "One nation under God." As America wrestled for its future, Benjamin Franklin wrote, "*... the little progress we have made in the last weeks is a melancholy proof of the imperfections of the human understanding, groping as it were in the dark. How has it happened that we have not sought the Father of lights to illuminate our understanding? In the beginning of the war with Britain we had daily prayer in this very room, and asked for divine protection. Our prayers were heard, and they were graciously answered. And have we now forgotten that powerful Friend? Or do we imagine that we no longer need His assistance? ... The longer I live, the more convincing proofs I see of this truth—that God governs in the affairs of men. And if a sparrow cannot fall to the ground without his notice, is it probable that an empire can rise without His aid? We have been assured in the sacred writings that 'except the Lord build the house they* *labor in vain that build it.' I therefore, beg leave to move, that hereafter prayers, imploring the assistance of Heaven and its blessings on our deliberations, be held in this assembly every morning before we proceed to business..."*

It is in this same spirit that a new, 21st Century-level of world-class intercession is arising. It is my sincere prayer that, after ingesting the truth revealed on every page of this timely and expertly crafted book, you too will be among those who answer the call to change the course of history through intercession.

Sher Valenzuela
Vice President
First State Manufacturing

Introduction

I live in Charlotte, North Carolina, but recently I have been spending a great deal of time in Delaware. The Lord told me that the bridge to connect these two places together was complete, and now I find myself traveling between the two states frequently. When I recently returned from a trip, as soon as my plane landed it seemed like everything was lined up in my favor. We landed right on time, the shuttle to long-term parking drove up just as I stepped out the door, and I was dropped off within a few feet of my car minutes later. The drive home was quick and painless. The ease of the flight, the drive, my car, and my house all seemed to be whispering, "Welcome home."

Charlotte is where I recharge. Family, church, and friends are what draw me back, and the Lord makes this place my safe harbor.

Delaware is where I am on constant alert. I can sense the spiritual battle being waged over the land and the people. When blizzards and hurricanes threaten to wipe Delaware off the map, the intercessor within me rises up and stands ground until the threat departs. When the local business owners, ministry leaders, and concerned citizens come under spiritual attack, the intercessor within me stands toe-to-toe with the demons trying to undermine everything they have worked for and says, "No." When churches asked for help training their intercessors to do the same, I said, "Yes!" So for the present time, I am leading an intercessor's charge over Delaware.

Back in the Day

Years ago, when women's coffees and prayer clubs were popular, true intercessors were rare. I am thankful that prayer and intercession have more relevance today, and Christian leaders on all the mountains of influence in society are beginning to understand the significance of their role. But even more important is the impact that can be felt when true intercession takes place that can safeguard a city and change the course of history in a nation.

I began prayer walking in the eighties in a small town in eastern Oregon. Back then, spiritual warfare was not widely understood or taught in our culture so I went around claiming the ground for Jesus, binding the devil, and knocking down strongholds without reservation. My family learned the hard way that intercessors who jump into battle without the Lord's blessing or strategy can experience serious demonic backlash. We saw major victories, but our family suffered, everyone I took with me suffered, and the churches in the area suffered. The warfare was intense. When we finally left the city, I think the people breathed a sigh of relief. Thankfully, the Lord showed me that we can move mountains through prayer and leave behind His favor and blessing if we follow His lead and intercede in His prescribed way.

About This Book

I have spent far more time learning the ways of the Lord than the devil's schemes. I am much more interested in what the Lord is doing than what Satan is doing. I am a worshipper and not a "ghost buster," and I don't waste my time thinking about the devil and blaming him for all our troubles. That being said, I am grateful for the truths the Lord has taught me about the role of the intercessor on the frontlines of battle. This book is simply the story of my journey and how I learned to wage effective spiritual warfare in the places He has taken me. Like many of you, I am in the process of learning and growing as an intercessor.

This book is my testimony. It is not meant to be an in-depth teaching on the subject of intercession, although I believe what is written here is true to the Scriptures. I have tried to communicate my experiences through the lens of my understanding of the Word of God. I have a practical but spiritual approach to life's lessons and believe the Lord speaks to us in many ways, including our experiences. My greatest desire is to live out my life as one who is crucified with Christ, but alive through faith in the Son of God (see Galatians 2:20). I believe in all of the gifts of the Spirit, especially the greatest gift of all—love.

Note: I have written about some of the significant people, places, and events that were an important part of my journey as an intercessor, but have changed some of the names, timeframes, and places to honor and protect their privacy.

Who are the World-Class Intercessors?

I do not think the world has seen the likes of these dread champions yet. They are the ones called to prepare the way for the Lord's return, the violent ones spoken of in Matthew 11:12, who are being raised up to take the kingdom by force. The Lord is calling His champions to the front lines of the battle to prepare the way for His return.

The Lord gave me a word concerning this new breed of intercessor that you will read about in Chapter 1. We are living in serious times. The world has need of fearless intercessors who will stand in the gap and declare the words the Lord is releasing in these dark days. It is a noble call and one I hope you will hear and respond to.

Standing in the gap with you!

Judy Sullivan

Part One

The Journey

CHAPTER 1

Who Are the Intercessors?

I praise you because I am fearfully and wonderfully made; your works are wonderful, I know that full well.

(Psalm 139:14)

The End of the Stereotype

She was one of the scary ones. When she said, "Oh you're an intercessor too!" I knew then and there I didn't like that title because I did not want to be like her. You know who I am talking about. She shows up at all the prayer meetings and tries to take over. Once she is in control, it is hard to get her to let go. She loves to dominate, because she is always right. She believes if you do not pray her way, there won't be a breakthrough. She corrects imperfect prayers with her declarations and pronounces her "Amens" with a blast from her shofar. She pushes all the right buttons, prays all the right words, and expects praise and accolades for all her efforts.

I sympathize with pastors who are nervous around certain intercessors, because they can be intimidating when they move in their gifts without discipline. If they operate from a carnal desire to be seen or heard, or if they use their gifts to control people, they are dangerously close to aligning with a witchcraft or Jezebel spirit. It is no wonder many churches fail to see intercession as a valuable ministry.

True intercessors are as varied and distinctive in their styles of prayer as prophets, musicians, preachers, and teachers are in their respective gifts. That's how God created us to be—different, creative, and unique. There are bold intercessors who rattle the walls with strong cries and decrees. There are reserved intercessors who quietly wait on the Lord and pray softly in their closets. There are gifted musicians and singers who can change the atmosphere and create an open heaven by their intercession in music. There are creative ones who dance, play the shofar, and twirl flags and banners doing battle in the heavens with prophetic acts. Some labor in prayer and give birth to new things with deep groaning and tears. The worshippers are the intercessors who are on their knees or faces caught up in the third heaven, oblivious to everything else in the room (that is usually where you'll find me). Depending on the circumstances, there is almost no right or wrong way. The key is to be who the Lord created you to be while submitting to the requirements and expectations of your pastors and leaders.

What is the difference between an intercessor and a person who prays? Most Christians pray, but they are not all intercessors. Intercession is a way to communicate with God, similar to prayer, but it goes much deeper. Typically when people pray, it is centered on very personal issues, whereas intercession is praying on behalf of those who cannot or do not pray for themselves. According to Merriam Webster the word intercede means to "intervene between parties with a view to reconciling differences; to mediate." An intercessor is one who stands in the gap on someone else's behalf and asks for Divine intervention.

When Abraham pleaded with God to spare Sodom, he was fulfilling the role of an intercessor (see Genesis 18:16-33). Moses was an intercessor when he pleaded with God for the lives of the Israelites after they created a golden calf and worshipped it (see Exodus 32). Jesus was the ultimate intercessor when He laid down His life to make a way for mankind to be reconciled to God.

An intercessor is someone who asks for God's mercy when judgment is deserved. They have answered the call of II Chronicles 7:14, **"If my people, who are called by my name, will humble themselves and pray and seek my face and turn from their wicked ways, then I will hear from heaven, and I will forgive their sin and will heal their land."**

Genuine intercessors are selfless individuals whose highest purpose is to lay down their lives for those they are praying for. With fervent prayer, they stand between a person or a place and anything that threatens to harm them. They identify with them by making requests on their behalf, pleading their cause, and warring over issues affecting them. They seek mercy and forgiveness for others, even when it is undeserved. Their prayers change the atmosphere, command the day, stir up the heavens, and send demons running. An intercessor understands that "it's not about me" but about the Lord, His love for mankind, and His redemptive plan.

Intercessors are the hidden ones who stand in the gap from their secret places of prayer, repenting on behalf of others, crying out to the Lord for intervention. When they pray in public, their prayers are rich and carry the authority of those who have waited in the secret place of the Most High God. Their focus is to please the Lord and serve Him with their whole hearts. They are alert and sober-minded because they know the real enemy is not people, but the devil who prowls around like a roaring lion looking for someone to devour (see I Peter 5:8). Their passion is to set the captives free so they can experience all of the Lord's goodness. Once we get past the hoopla and stereotypes, it is truly a noble calling. I challenge you to ask the Lord who you are. Find out if you are one of the hidden ones, a world-class intercessor in the making.

Who Am I?

I met the Lord when I was a child and attended church most of my life, but my relationship with Him was limited. It wasn't until I was a young adult that my need for Him increased, and I discovered His love for me on a deeply personal level. Without planning to, I had encountered what Scripture calls the "baptism of the Holy Spirit," including all the spiritual gifts mentioned in I Corinthians chapters 12 to 14. My love for the Word increased dramatically after that life-transforming experience and so did my love for the Lord and everyone around me. I had dreams and visions in full color. Eventually I learned to understand what the Lord was saying to me through these experiences and apply them to my life and my understanding of Scripture. I saw things in dreams that helped me understand how to pray effective prayers for others. I began to see situations from heaven's viewpoint and stand in the gap as a prayer warrior on behalf of others. The Lord was infusing my spirit with the DNA of an intercessor.

There are a lot of books and teachings saturating the body of Christ today about discovering who we are. *The Purpose Driven Life*, by Rick Warren, Lance Wallnau's 7 Mountain teachings, and the myriads of material that the Lord is releasing through others on the subject are leading the charge. Understanding what mountain we're called to, knowing why we were created, and what we are supposed to be doing during our short lifespan has been nothing short of an "awakening" in the church. Life without purpose is reckless and pointless. Scripture agrees, **"Where there is no vision, the people perish"** (see Proverbs 29:18 KJV).

The devil knows this all too well. His attacks on the body of Christ are aimed at the very heart and foundation of our identity, because he knows if we were to walk confidently knowing who we are, there would be no stopping us. As intercessors, knowing who we are in the Lord is the key to fulfilling our roles. Once we understand our role, our prayers will take on a new level of authority and all things will become possible. Imagine what can happen when the people you pray for start to see who they really are.

Recently I was on a phone call with a group of politically invested people. One of the women on the call asked us to pray about a job offer she was considering. As I prayed for her, I saw she was much larger on the inside than on the outside. There were embers of life beginning to burn that she was just becoming aware of. Then I saw she was like a large smoke stack on a ship, giving power to the entire ship. A smokestack has no means of giving power, but in the vision, it represented the engine powering the ship. I could see she had a call on her life to bring power and direction to something very big. As I shared this vision with her, I prayed, "Lord, help her to see who she is." I encouraged her to make certain that her decision lined up with her true calling and identity. When I shared this insight with her, the decision became easier. Now she is well on her way to fulfilling her calling to the governmental mountain.

You have probably heard the phrase, "The mind is a terrible thing to waste." I would take that a step further and say, "A life is a terrible thing to waste." We were born for a purpose. God did not create a world of puppets. We are created in His image with wonderful minds and bodies. We possess everything we need to accomplish extraordinary things in this life. God placed us on this earth to tend and care for it. He has given us His Word for instruction in His ways, His Holy Spirit to counsel and guide us, and our physical bodies to walk out His will and purposes on the earth.

Understanding who we are as intercessors is foundational to everything else we do. If we are confused about our identity, we will be unfocused and undisciplined in everything. Our best efforts will be half-hearted because we won't really know where we are going or why we are doing it.

Personality Tests and God-Encounters

Most of us have jobs or titles that define our role in society. But these are not who we are, they are what we do as a result of who we are. You may have been through one of the many personality tests circulating the church and marketplace today. I have taken several, and each time I have learned something new about myself. These are great tools that I often recommend to marketplace leaders. They serve a purpose in helping people identify what they are good at and not so good at, and what personality type they work well with. But like all systematic approaches to life, these can overlook the "God factor."

Contrary to popular opinion, God's call on our lives rarely fits our personality profile. Scripture tells us David was anointed to be a king when he was a child, but he was the least likely candidate in his family. Moses was God's chosen deliverer but he couldn't speak clearly. Gideon was called a mighty warrior while hiding in a wine press. Simon was anything but a rock, but Jesus called him Peter, which when translated means "rock." Their true identities were not evident when the Lord called them. They all would have failed a test for courage, because it was the anointing that made them brave. I often wonder how they would have fared in a personality test. Would they have been locked into a future that missed the mark for their true identity?

Mary, the mother of Jesus, was a simple girl whose plans for her future probably were not much bigger than mine were at her age, but when she had a God-encounter everything changed. Gabriel did not make her take a personality test before announcing she would be the most important mother of all time. She probably did not fit the profile for the demands of such a high calling by today's standards. It takes a God-encounter to make us into the people we were born to be.

Embrace the Process

When we realize who we are, even though we are still in the process of getting there, our confidence will grow. We may not be world-class intercessors yet, but like so many who have gone before us, God calls those things that are not as though they were (see Romans 4:17).

We are known and identified by a combination of things. Outwardly, we are known by our appearances—how we walk and talk. Inwardly, we are known by our personality and emotions. Our cultures play a huge role in making us who we are. The era we grew up in marked us. The churches we attended helped to define our character. In many ways, we mirror our parents and siblings. All of our history has played a vibrant role in forming our identities. Not one moment of our lives will be wasted. It is all part of who we are.

We are a product of our bloodline, environment, culture, and spiritual heritage. When the Lord calls us, He does not wipe out our history. He uses every bit of it to create an entirely new creation in Christ. Everything we have been through is used to form us into His image and to bring out our true calling. Every mistake we have made and every sin we have committed will become the bedding soil the Lord uses to grow His character in our lives. One of the miracles of His forgiveness is we will discover who we were meant to be. Life's hard lessons will leave a mark in our spiritual DNA, giving us greater authority in the very places the enemy had used against us.

Guard Your Identity!

Our identity is our inheritance, our birthright. Esau sold his birthright for a morsel of bread. The prodigal son squandered his for a few moments of pleasure. If we sell our birthright, we are giving our identities to another. The Bible cautions us in Revelation 3:11 to hold on to what we have so no one will take our crown. Once we discover who we are, we must guard our identity as if it were the greatest treasure on earth. Consider this sober warning, **"See that no one is sexually immoral, or is godless like Esau, who for a single meal sold his inheritance rights as the oldest son. Afterward, as you know, when he wanted to inherit this blessing, he was rejected. Even though he sought the blessing with tears, he could not change what he had done" (Hebrews 12:16-17).**

When the Lord calls us out of darkness into His marvelous light, all of our life experiences, everything that has gone into making us who we are is miraculously transformed. Like the butterfly emerging out of a cocoon, we are much more beautiful than we thought we were. If we press in and listen closely, the Lord will tell us who we really are. Understanding our true identity and knowing what our birthright is will keep us focused and in the right place, doing the right thing.

Intercessors do not need a title or degree to enter this God-ordained calling. There is not a certain personality type that is the best fit for the role. A new breed of intercessor is emerging from the ash heap of trials and testing. Like true pioneers, we have learned things the hard way, and we have been humbled by our mistakes. Standing on the front lines of the battle has taught us that the Greater One lives inside, so when the conflict of the ages begins, we will be brave.

Hold On To Your Hats!

The Lord spoke the following word to me recently concerning this new breed of intercessor. This is the premise from which now flows all God has called me to do. I hope it will encourage you as it encourages me.

"Get ready for I am about to blow through ceilings and crash through doors and turn the enemy on his butt. I am bringing you into high places that will defy all logic and shatter the mindsets of the skeptics. I am making you into world-class intercessors for just these days. You will witness the changing of structures and weather patterns, kingdoms will rise and fall, presidents and world leaders will hear My voice through you and respond. I am removing the veil that has hidden you and bringing you to the top of the elevator where you will see and be seen. Fear not, little ones, it is not because of you I do this. It is because of the hour at hand that I am raising up world-class intercessors to stand in the gap and speak forth My prayers so the world and its realm will obey My commands. Hang on! This is going to be a wild ride. It will defy your own logical sense of how things should be. Drop the religious spirit and hold

onto your hats. You are about to be shot out like cannons from your resting place."

The Lord is waking up His intercessors. It is an exciting time to be alive! My prayer is that this book will help you recognize who you are and give you the courage to do what you are called to do. It is a noble calling, and though we may have missed opportunities or worn out our welcome in the past, God is the God of second chances. He is hitting the reset button now, and we have the incredible opportunity to get it right this time!

I did not always know I was called to be an intercessor. I spent many years running from my calling and learning things the hard way. The price I paid for understanding authority in prayer was great and came through family crises, the loss of my husband, and a move across the country far from my home and loved ones. I learned about spiritual warfare when I was young and naïve and dabbled in the occult. Playing with fire will get you burned no matter how innocent you are. I learned a great deal about deliverance, spiritual warfare, and discernment in the process. But I am getting ahead of myself. Let me tell you how it started.

Chapter 2

My Story

For I am the Lord your God who takes hold of your right hand and says to you, do not fear, I will help you.

(Isaiah 41:13 NIV)

School Days

"Judy, your skirt is too short." The counselor smiled as she handed me a pink slip. Girls in high school were not allowed to wear pants or jeans in the sixties, so our skirts had to touch the ground when we knelt down. Minutes later, a boy with shaggy hair was spotted, "Get a haircut! I can't see the top of your ears." The counselor was handing out pink slips left and right to the mass of kids dashing to first period. Parents would be notified and expected to dole out the appropriate punishment from home. No TV, no phone calls, and grounded for a week. That was enough to straighten out most of us. The real delinquents who were caught smoking in the bathroom would be doing detention.

I remember praying the Lord's Prayer in the first grade. We didn't have a flag in our classroom, so we recited the words from Luke 11:2-4, **"Our Father who art in heaven, hallowed be Thy name. Thy kingdom come, Thy will be done, on earth as it is in heaven..." (KJV).** Just a few short years later, school prayer was outlawed, and "God is dead" became the iconic symbol for the rebellious and ever more secular sixties.

The change in American values from the fifties to the sixties was drastic. Many stay-at-home moms traded in their aprons for typewriters and steno pads, while their kids came home to empty houses with less rules and more freedom. They could afford bigger houses with swimming pools, a second car, and regular vacations. Who could argue with that? You've heard the familiar adage, "When the cat's away the mice will play?" But for many, the added income was worth it, and in many cases, desperately needed.

My moral compass had been set in stone early, so when Mom returned to work, it was only for a few hours in the afternoon. I came home from school to a list of chores and learned to cook, sew, and clean house like a pro. Since we were only allowed a few hours of approved TV a week, Friday nights were reserved for family time. Instead of movie nights like most family time in the 21st century, we had game nights. Mom made the best spaghetti and apple pie on the planet, and when we weren't playing board games, Dad taught us how to play poker. It was an interesting combination, but Dad was a strategist and wanted us to learn his techniques.

The sixties were embroiled with hot-button issues like the Vietnam War, women's rights, and civil rights. The availability of "the pill" as an effective form of birth control ushered in the sexual revolution. Marijuana use as a recreational drug was exploding in high schools and on college campuses. All this served to accelerate a breakdown in the family and amplify disrespect for authority.

I think families that maintained strong ties and values fared better in the turbulent sixties than most. When the hippies started showing up with their "make love, not war" signs and peace symbols, it never occurred to me that engaging in their lifestyle was an option. Drugs, sex, and alcohol were not even on my radar. Oh sure, I rocked the boat occasionally, and my parents had to put me on restriction from time to time, but I don't think I caused them too many sleepless nights.

As I look back on those years, I wonder where the intercessors were. Many of us who are old enough to remember were intercessors in the making, but not ready to stand in the gap and turn back the evil that was crouching at our door. The times we live in now are more perilous because our nation has forgotten its heritage. We can't turn back the clock, but we can remember what we once were, recognize evil for what it is, and call our nation back to its rightful place.

My Spiritual Journey

My parents attended church occasionally during my childhood, but my brother Jim and I went to Sunday school on a regular basis. Mom was a believer and made sure we were learning about God on Sundays. Since Dad was an agnostic, he rarely went with us and Mom would not go without him. I was a young preteen when we went to a Billy Graham Crusade in Los Angeles. During the altar call, while the choir sang "Just As I Am", Mom, Jim and I went forward, confessed our sins, and gave our hearts to the Lord. After that I started attending the Baptist church a few miles from home with a girlfriend and her family. My parents would join me there occasionally, but we all considered it my church. Jim was moving on in life, excelling in school, and church took a backseat.

I fell in love with Tim in high school. He was everything I was looking for in a prospective husband. He was good looking, intelligent, athletic, and had a strong moral character. He was also a lot of fun and had a great sense of humor. His family was simply the happiest, most enjoyable people I had ever known. I enjoyed my family too, but they rarely went anywhere and didn't socialize much. Tim's family members, on the other hand, were social butterflies. They loved outings and gatherings, and they went on vacations every year. Whenever I was at their home, I was always part of the family. They invited me to stay for dinner almost every night. I went with them to visit their friends. Occasionally I was even invited to go on trips with them.

Deception

It was late one summer night when Tim pulled the car up to the curb following dinner, "I've got something to tell you, Judy." He was rarely this somber, and he had my full attention. When I turned to say good night, I immediately sensed an unusual seriousness in his tone. "My family has its own religion—a kind of church, but not the same as you're used to." I settled back in my seat and waited for him to continue. "It's a spiritualist church. You know, where people go for séances and talk to their dead relatives." I hadn't heard of that denomination before and was fascinated as he explained that his family participated in séances. "We have a church in Apple Valley that we go to every month. Our friends, Mary and Fred, are the pastors." That was really outside of my frame of reference, but I listened politely. "Do you want to come with us to church next Sunday?" My eyes widened in disbelief that this intelligent, handsome, young man and his equally bright family were hardcore followers of something that I thought was reserved for scaring ourselves at slumber parties. But I was in love with Tim and his family, and any time there was an opportunity to be with them, I was ready to go.

"Absolutely not!" Dad's reaction was predictable. It wasn't because he didn't want me to be with the spiritualists—it was inappropriate for a young girl to be traveling overnight with a boy, even though I would be with his family.

Mom pulled out her Bible and started showing me Scriptures about spiritualism and witchcraft and how it was a sin against God to participate in such things.

Dad switched tracks and replied with mild irritation, "It's harmless. God doesn't care about their misguided beliefs." Whenever Dad talked about God, I knew he was just trying to pacify Mom. Somehow their differences in opinion cancelled each other out, and in the end, they let me go.

Little did I know that something far more insidious than enjoying the pleasures of sin for a season was being offered to me by the deceiver. I may have avoided the pitfalls of moral failure that many of my peers fell into, but this was a much bigger trap. The devil used my naivety to open a floodgate of deception that would shake up my faith and attempt to derail my future calling as an intercessor.

A Mountain of Evidence

Mary and Fred were an older couple who lived in an amazing old house filled with trinkets, books, and all sorts of occult doodads. It was evident the moment we walked through the door that Tim's family adored them. As people started showing up, I was surprised that these normal-looking, intelligent people believed in things like Ouija boards, crystal balls, and tarot cards.

My first real encounter with the demonic world began that night when Fred turned off the lights, and everyone sat around in a tight circle. Fred gave us a few instructions, "I want everyone to lay your hands face up on your laps, and don't cross your arms or your legs."

Tim whispered an explanation in my ear, "We are creating a battery of light that will draw spirits into our circle."

"Oh, great," I groaned under my breath. I was very skeptical, but also very afraid. I ignored the instructions and grabbed hold of Tim's arm and waited to see what would happen next.

Before turning out the lights, Fred placed a black cone they called a "trumpet" on the floor in the center of our circle. The room was completely dark, the windows had been boarded up, and every source of light had been covered. Then the trumpet started speaking. Even though I couldn't see it, I could tell it was circling the room, moving in front of each person, and speaking to them. Tim patted my arm to reassure me as the trumpet paused in front of me.

Then something touched me from behind like a strong puff of wind. The hair on the back of my neck stood straight up, and everything in me wanted to run out of the room. "Is Mary holding the trumpet?" I blurted out. A few people laughed, but I was able to maintain my composure long enough to see a green light appear over Mary as she took over or something took her over. The voice coming through the trumpet was now coming through her.

Tim continued to reassure me, "Mary's spirit has gone on a flight. She isn't here now."

At that moment, the trumpet dropped to the floor, and on the opposite side of the room a strong male voice came booming through Mary's vocal cords. "This is Dr. Beel!" Everyone in the room took a deep breath and waited expectantly for what he was about to say. "I'm here to give you instruction from The Bible." He proceeded to teach and instruct us through Mary's voice and body. I don't remember much about his lengthy sermon because it wasn't anything to write home about. But I was beginning to understand what a spiritualist church was all about. It wasn't until years later that I learned that the devil not only knows The Bible, but he uses it to trap people into believing his distorted version of the truth.

After the séance, fear became my daily companion. What I had seen and heard were far more real than I had expected. Dad said, "It's all smoke and mirrors! They're just misguided people with big imaginations."

Mom kept quoting Scriptures from Deuteronomy, especially the ones about detestable practices, "Let no one be found among you who consults mediums or spiritists!"

Dad was a man of few words, "Nonsense!"

Nevertheless, I continued visiting the Apple Valley church and witnessed even greater deception. Rocks materialized from thin air, prophecies were told and fulfilled, healings took place, and spirits spoke in foreign languages through Mary that she could not have known. Tim told me that once a police officer came with the intent of exposing Mary and Fred as fakes, but when he turned on his flashlight to reveal whatever he was expecting to find, his flashlight batteries had mysteriously disappeared. Needless to say he was a "believer" when he left.

A few months later, Mary and Fred came to Tim's family home to setup shop there for a small but growing following of their friends. Everything proceeded in the usual way, including my ignoring the instructions for the proper way to sit. I held on to Tim's arm in fear, waiting for things to fire up. This particular night, Tim's best friend Mike was there. He was as skeptical as I had been on my first encounter with these strange experiences.

Almost immediately, a new voice from the "other side" began talking through Mary. This one sounded like a frightened young man. "Please, can somebody help me?" He didn't seem to know where he was, but he recognized Mike and spoke to him. "Mike, where am I?"

Mike seemed to know him, "He's in the military, fighting in Vietnam."

The fact that this young man was speaking to him from the "other side" was evidence to the group that he had died in battle, something that had not yet been reported. But even stranger was that this kid did not know where he was or that he was dead.

Tim's mother explained, "His spirit is wandering the earth plain, and he doesn't know what happened to him or where he is."

Tim's family and the other regulars in the group knew what to do. They called out to him, "Come to the light!"

Then Tim explained to Mike and me, "Our circle is creating a light that will direct him on to his new plain of existence."

Seconds later, he cried out, "Oh my God, there's my mother!" and disappeared.

I don't remember much else from that night. Mike was visibly shaken. Within a few days, our suspicions were confirmed. His friend had died in battle about the time we were having our séance. If there had been any skepticism left in me, it was gone after this. This was not just smoke and mirrors. This was as real as you can get. But for my part, it was scary enough that I never attended another séance. The Lord protected me even though I didn't know I needed protection.

It is not possible to combine Christianity with spiritualism because spiritualism contradicts the most basic foundational truths in Scripture. Spiritists believed in Jesus, and some even called themselves Christians, but to them, Jesus was just one of many great teachers and not the Son of God who died for their sins. They based their religion on a few Scriptures, but they didn't understand the message of salvation through Jesus' death or the power of His blood, and they rationalized the warnings about spiritism in the Old Testament.

The fundamentalist church I attended preached salvation but knew nothing about the power and authority of the cross or the gifts of the Spirit. I had seen unexplainable paranormal events take place, but no one in my church could explain what I had witnessed. My pastor thought people who did such things were just confused, and it wasn't real or anything to be worried about. I continued to go to my church, sing in the choir, and attend youth group, but I had changed. I was no longer a fun-loving teenager. I had become fearful and confused. I didn't understand it then, but I had encountered the "angel of light" spoken of in II Corinthians 11:14, a strong satanic deception that took years for me to recognize and overcome.

A New Chapter

Tim attended church with me and went through the motions of professing faith in Jesus and being baptized. He didn't renounce his spiritualist roots because he didn't see anything wrong with the family religion. After two years in our local college, he was accepted to a university in Utah where five more years of school and two degrees awaited him. Since he didn't want to leave me behind, we married, and moved to Logan, Utah where a new chapter in our lives began.

We lived in Logan for five years, where 95% of the residents were Mormon. We attended a Presbyterian church and became youth group leaders. Somehow we managed to have two children during the time Tim was getting his Bachelors and Masters Degrees, and I worked and grabbed a few college courses in my spare time.

We had many Latter Day Saint (LDS) friends, but we considered it our duty to make sure we weren't mistaken for followers of their faith. So we drank coffee in public, I wore shorts and sleeveless blouses, and Tim swore regularly and drank beer. It was the beer drinking that got us noticed by concerned Christians who suggested that drinking was a poor witness to our Mormon friends. Their concern bothered me more than it did Tim, but it got me back into The Bible and praying again.

Tim continued to go to séances with his family whenever we were in California. This disturbed me a great deal because I felt an evil associated with it I could not explain. During our final year at Utah State University, I began seeking answers again about the things I had experienced. My pastor tried to reassure me, "Everyone has a different way of worshiping God. Don't let it worry you." But our Christian friends who said drinking was a poor witness, actually had answers I could understand. They explained, "All supernatural experiences are not necessarily from God. The devil has power too!" I grew up in church, so I just assumed all supernatural experiences were from God, even though I had never seen that kind of power in my church.

Our friends gave me a book called *Pigs in the Parlor* by Frank and Ida Mae Hammond. I wouldn't recommend this for bedtime reading, but it finally shed some light on what we were dealing with. Spiritualism, or more accurately spiritism, because there's nothing spiritual about it, is the oldest counterfeit religion known to man. My mom was right all along, and now the Scriptures she had been trying to show me suddenly made sense. I discovered that The Bible had a lot to say about it. I had been deceived by looking at people instead of the Scriptures. In my naivety, I assumed good people wouldn't be involved with anything bad. I believed physical evidence and demonstrations of power automatically made these experiences real and from God, but that was the ultimate deception. Here is what The Bible has to say about it:

> **"Do not turn to mediums or necromancers; do not seek them out, and so make yourselves unclean by them: I am the Lord your God" (Leviticus 19:31 ESV).**

> **"There shall not be found among you anyone who burns his son or his daughter as an offering, anyone who practices divination or tells fortunes or interprets omens, or a sorcerer or a charmer or a medium or a necromancer or one who inquires of the dead, for whoever does these things is an abomination to the Lord. And because of these abominations the Lord your God is driving them out before you" (Deuteronomy 18:10-12 ESV).**

> **"Beloved, do not believe every spirit, but test the spirits to see whether they are from God, for many false prophets have gone**

out into the world" (I John 4:1 ESV).

"Now the Spirit expressly says that in later times some will depart from the faith by devoting themselves to deceitful spirits and teachings of demons" (I Timothy 4:1 ESV).

"So Saul died for his breach of faith. He broke faith with the Lord in that he did not keep the command of the Lord, and also consulted a medium, seeking guidance" (I Chronicles 10:13 ESV).

I realized that by participating in séances I had broken faith with the Lord. He was no longer my covering, and without His protection, I had come under a strong satanic delusion. When we are walking with the Lord, we should be walking in greater peace, experiencing His blessings, and increasing in love. If we are walking in the opposite spirit, fear, anxiety, and hopelessness will increase and eventually lead to greater deception and evil (see James 3:16).

I repented and renounced my involvement with the occult and rededicated my life to the Lord. My fear of the dark was replaced with a deep love for the Lord and a hunger for His Word. Over time, I learned to recognize deception in its various forms by learning more about the Lord and feeding on His Word. True discernment comes from knowing the Truth so well that when a counterfeit surfaces, we recognize it immediately.

Moving On

Shortly after graduation, Tim took his first real job in Jackson, Wyoming. We packed up our two children and our meager belongings and moved to our first assignment with the Forest Service. It was in this beautiful setting near the Grand Tetons and Yellowstone National Park that one summer morning Tim dropped to his knees and repented for his involvement in the occult. He was wonderfully saved, set free, and delivered to a new life in the Lord. The years of "dancing with the devil" made a deep mark in his life, and he had more battles to fight, but Jackson was a place of many miracles for both of us. This was where we were filled with the Spirit and learned to move in the gifts recorded in I Corinthians chapters 12 and 14. We learned about spiritual warfare firsthand because we had to break off the demonic ties and inroads into our lives. We had been toe-to-toe with the devil and had learned a great deal about his deceptive tactics in the process. The Lord was preparing us for what was ahead.

If you will look back over your life experiences, you will see the hand of the Lord directing your path and equipping you for each assignment. Our next assignment was a roller coaster ride that we felt scarcely ready for. If I only knew then what I know now, I would have avoided that lesson. I am thankful the Lord will even use our immaturity to lay down important foundations. Oregon is where that happened for us.

CHAPTER 3

The Battleground

I rise before dawn and cry for help;
I have put my hope in your word.

(Psalm 119:147 NIV)

The Battle Over Central Oregon

"We're moving to Oregon!" After five years in Jackson, Wyoming, Tim was ready for the next step in his career, so it was time to pack up and move again. Everyone called it God's country, and we couldn't wait to get there. Tim's new office was in a thriving city with a population of 2,000. Our home was a mile up the road nestled in the mountains of central Oregon. This idyllic place to "get away from it all" and raise a family had the added benefit of being at least two and a half hours from the nearest McDonalds or shopping center. To get anywhere in any direction, we had to travel through mountain ranges lined with logging trucks, cattle drives, and for a brief time when we lived there, the Rajneeshees. You may have heard of them.

Bhagwan Shree Rajneesh, a hostile opponent of traditional eastern religion and an outspoken critic of Mahatma Gandhi, was a controversial character from India. His open attitude towards sexuality earned him the title of "sex guru" in the international press. In 1970, he took on the role of a spiritual leader and began making disciples. In 1981, he moved his growing flock of followers to the United States near our little neck of the woods and established a commune known as Rajneeshpuram, located eighteen miles from Antelope and about ninety miles from our home. In a city where you had to drive two and a half hours for a Big Mac, they were practically our next-door neighbors.

According to Ward Tonsfeldt and Paul G. Claeyssens (2004) authors of *The Oregon History Project, Post-Industrial Years: 1970-Present: Communities in the Post-Industrial Period*: **(ohs.org/education/oregonhistory/narratives/subtopic.cfm?subtopic_id=414)**

> "Although all central Oregon communities have undergone rapid changes, none has been more profoundly affected by the new times than the tiny ranching town of Antelope. In June 1981, followers of Indian guru Bhagwan Shree Rashneesh purchased the 64,000 acre Big Muddy Ranch near Antelope for $5.7 million, establishing a community they called Rashneeshpuram. The Rashneeshees, as they were known, gained

> control of the Antelope City Council in 1984 and changed the name of Antelope to Rashneesh. In August 1984, the sect began bussing homeless people from other U.S. cities to Rashneeshpuram, and registering them as Wasco County voters. After a series of bizarre incidents including an alleged attempt to poison residents of The Dalles, the Bhagwan and some of his followers fled to North Carolina. There he was arrested on charges of immigration fraud and was brought back to Oregon for trial. He was convicted, fined $400,000, and deported from the United States. The faithful accompanied the Bhagwan back to Pune, India, the homeless drifted away, the ranch was sold to new owners, and life eventually returned to normal in Antelope, which got its old name back in 1986."

We knew there was trouble in paradise when Rajneesh's followers started showing up wearing maroon "pajamas," shopping in our stores, eating our food, and making their presence known. With just one hardware store, one barber shop, two grocery stores, and churches on every other corner, this was an invasion worthy of notice. There were up to 7,000 followers living in the commune, and when they came to town, everything came to a screeching halt. Prayer warriors all across Oregon started calling out to the Lord for deliverance. Their proximity to our cities was alarming. Given their numbers, they had the ability to literally take over our town and use our laws against us. The thought of their foreign gods infesting our communities and our children was beyond comprehension.

Even though there were numerous churches in our city, there wasn't a deep need for God's intervention until now. Few understood spiritual warfare at the time. My husband and I were labeled "extreme" because I prayer walked our neighborhood, and we occasionally prayed deliverance prayers for oppressed people. Small traditional churches where drums were considered radical and preachers with new ideas didn't last long were the norm. Unity between denominations was unheard of, and mistrust and jealousy between believers was the order of the day.

In this setting, the Lord told me to start a prayer ministry. Tim and I called the people to pray from one end of the state to the other. We hosted concerts of prayer, prayer watches, prayer breakfasts, and pioneered prayer walking efforts. In the aftermath, our pastor accused us of rebellion, not submitting to his authority, and asked us to leave. This was the low point in our short prayer ministry, but the burden to press on kept us going.

Rajneeshpuram

Our family took an annual road trip to Warm Beach, Washington the summer of 1985 to attend a Christian family camp. With 3 children, camping gear, and luggage all crammed inside and on top of our car, we must have been quite a sight. We got a lot of stares from people passing us on the road. I heard something about *National Lampoon's Summer Vacation* when we stopped for gas and decided it was a fair comparison. Our children were still small, but our daughter rolled her eyes and groaned with embarrassment. Tim was tall and lanky, and with his brown hair and sideburns, he bore a remarkable resemblance to Chevy Chase. He was totally oblivious to it all, but on the way home it would prove to be useful.

In Tim's position as the Forest Soil Scientist, he had access to road maps in Oregon that the average person never saw. He knew the back road into the Big Muddy Ranch, the location of Rajneeshpuram and the home of Bhagwan Shree Rajneesh and his 7,000 followers. He decided on our way home that we would drive through the commune. I was a little nervous to say the least when we left the paved road and entered the "forbidden" territory that was operated by men and women who wore maroon and chanted. We had no idea what to expect.

The dirt road was well kept, but it was also well guarded. We passed guard towers and people with guns, but not one of them attempted to stop us from entering the commune. Why would they? We looked like Chevy Chase and his sweet family taking a vacation. I turned around and looked sternly at the kids, "Start praying!" We all put our hands on the windows and prayed like there was no tomorrow. Our sweet family on vacation was far more of a threat to them with our prayers and petitions than they were with their guns and demonic chants.

We passed Tent City where hundreds of small tents were neatly lined up in rows across a large flat area. We saw the infamous collection of Rolls-Royces and the airstrip for Bhagwan's private fleet of jets. The city itself had a fire department, restaurants, shopping center, townhouses, public transportation, and a post office with a ZIP code. Not what I expected from a spiritual fanatic. We kept praying as we drove in and around the streets. The people troubled me. They all looked vacant and mindless as they walked through their city. They were a mixture of ethnic backgrounds, but most were white Americans. It was hard to imagine doctors, lawyers, and other professionals giving away their entire life savings and abandoning families and careers for this lifestyle. I am sure we were stared at and talked about for days afterwards.

On the other side of the commune, we decided we did not want to turn around and drive back through because it would have added a couple of hours to our drive home. Instead we picked up the dirt road on the other side and prayed that it went through and connected to the main road. Tim was fairly certain it did, and since he was an adventurer at heart, he wanted to give it a shot. On the other hand, I was getting more nervous as I watched the sun disappear over the mountains, knowing we had no idea where we were, and we certainly did not want to spend the night in Rajneeshpuram. Thinking back, I am pretty sure Tim knew what he was doing all along, but he was enjoying the thrill of the adventure.

We made it home, and within a few days the adventure was a fading memory. That is until less than a week later when we read in the paper that Bhagwan was arrested on charges of immigration fraud and deported, and the commune had collapsed. We could not help but ask ourselves, did our prayers have anything to do with it, and did the prayers of all those intercessors in central Oregon make a difference?

This One's Too Big For You

Spiritual warfare was a fairly new concept in the eighties. There were not many books on the subject until Frank Peretti's book, *This Present Darkness*, came out in 1986 and shed light on the reality of demons, angels, and the spiritual battle surrounding us. Most believers knew of the devil and would even casually joke when they did something wrong, "The devil made me do it," but few understood the impact demons have on the world in which we live.

We lived in Oregon for nearly twelve years. It was a learning time, but it was also one of the most difficult times in our lives. We were making inroads into the Department of Education, attending their meetings and reviewing books that were under-considered for distribution in the schools. In the process, we discovered they were adding alternate sex-themed curriculum to the elementary, junior, and senior high schools. This was a radical shift from their usual curriculum, and we called upon the community to respond. We started a prayer vigil and began calling down the stronghold. Tim and I were praying together in our living room at that time when Tim heard the Lord distinctly say, "This one's too big for you." We were shocked because we had never backed down from spiritual warfare prayers. Why would the Lord say this? Didn't we have all authority? Didn't Scripture say to cast out demons and tread on scorpions (see Luke 10:19)? Apparently, there was a lot more to it as we were beginning to learn. Our growing concern was the negative impact all this was having on our family, particularly our daughter.

She was our blue-eyed treasure, our first born, and the subject of all our parenting blunders. She was the classic strong-willed child that makes parents want to turn in their parent buttons and cry, "Uncle!" But we were armed with Dr. Dobson's book, *The Strong-Willed Child*, surrounded ourselves with wise counsel, and prayed a lot. At the same time, we were on the front lines of battle in the schools, picketing liberal senators who opposed the right to life, leading prayer vigils, and marching for Jesus. That was when our beautiful daughter came under a horrific attack. We watched her deteriorate from a happy, loving child to a sullen, despondent pre-teen. Within a year, she was in full-blown rebellion and closing in on a self-destructive lifestyle. Our hearts were broken, and we dropped everything to try and rescue her.

We were facing battles in the school, church, work, and our personal lives. It was an all-out war, and we were the targets. These were the issues that made us step back and examine our lives and our calling. Did we enter into a spiritual realm too big for us? Many of the attacks we were experiencing mirrored the issues we were dealing with.

I believe we were part of a new breed of prayer warriors who had entered into the battlefield. This was new territory, but it was also a new thing God was doing at the time. We were becoming the warrior bride with combat boots, but like all new things, we were blazing the trail and learning everything through trial and error. We saw prayer take down Rajneeshpuram and stop them from overrunning our cities and taking root in our state. However, understanding authority in prayer made us effective prayer warriors in some areas, but often put us in danger in others.

The Stronghold

I had a dream during that timeframe which the Lord used to help me understand and answer some of these questions. In the dream, I was in an enemy stronghold. It was surrounded with walls and towers, positioned above the earth where vision was unimpeded. In those years, I envisioned demonic strongholds below the earth, but the stronghold in my dream was above the earth, where the prince of the power of the air resides and rules (see Ephesians 2:2 KJV). I was only there as an observer and not in any danger. I saw large beings, wearing long cloaks with hoods giving all their attention to plotting out their attack. They were positioned all over the stronghold, working on what looked like round TV screens with green fluorescent gridlines, using fine precision tools to mark out their strategy. I was fascinated by the degree of planning and accuracy that went into locating their targets.

I had been taught demons were foolish creatures that were more afraid of us than we were of them. I think that is true of many ground level demons that stalk and torment people, but territorial spirits who rule over geographical regions seemed to be different. Ephesians 6:12 addresses this demonic hierarchy, **"For our struggle is not against flesh and blood, but against the rulers, against the authorities, against the powers of this dark world and against the spiritual forces of evil in the heavenly realms" (NIV)**.

Back to my dream: Every so often a cannonball would fly over the walls of the stronghold and land on the floor. The floor was completely covered with large cannonballs. Interestingly no one even noticed the floor or the cannonballs flying in. They were totally ineffective and didn't even slow things down. If anything, they served more to help the spiritual forces of evil get a fix on their targets. When I woke up, the Lord spoke to my spirit that in order to be effective in spiritual warfare, we needed to have a better strategy than the enemy.

Lessons from the Battle of Jericho

Joshua chapters 1 through 6 describe the first battle the Israelites fought in their conquest of the Promised Land. They were given strict instructions to prepare themselves before the battle and to engage in an unconventional strategy for taking the city of Jericho. We can glean important information from these chapters to help us be battle-ready and successful in spiritual warfare. This is not meant to be an in-depth study, so you may want to read through these Scriptures as a reference.

Deal with sin in the camp first: Joshua 3:5, **"And Joshua said to the people, 'Sanctify yourselves, for tomorrow the LORD will do wonders among you'" (NKJV).** According to Merriam Webster, to be sanctified means "to set apart to a sacred purpose or to religious use; to be free from sin." We must have clean hands and pure undivided hearts when entering into any spiritual battle. Our level of success is often determined by our level of freedom from sin. Set the bar high and deal with any sin not repented of before entering any spiritual battle so that the works of the flesh will not become a snare for the enemy to take advantage of. **"The acts of the flesh are obvious: sexual immorality, impurity and debauchery; idolatry and witchcraft; hatred, discord, jealousy, fits of rage, selfish ambition, dissensions, factions and envy; drunkenness, orgies, and the like. I warn you, as I did before, that those who live like this will not inherit the kingdom of God" (Galatians 5:19-21 NIV).**

Your promised land is holy: **"The commander of the LORD's army replied, 'Take off your sandals, for the place where you are standing is holy.' And Joshua did so" (Joshua 5:15 NIV).**

When the Lord leads us to our promised land, it is a sacred call with a holy purpose and we must treat the land that He is giving us as holy.

Get your marching orders from the Lord: "**March around the city once with all the armed men. Do this for six days. Have seven priests carry trumpets of rams' horns in front of the ark. On the seventh day, march around the city seven times, with the priests blowing the trumpets. When you hear them sound a long blast on the trumpets, have the whole army give a loud shout; then the wall of the city will collapse and the army will go up, everyone straight in" (Joshua 6:3-5 NIV).**

The different stages of this battle plan were important, but the most significant part of this plan was that Joshua received his marching orders from the Lord. It is vital we receive our strategy and direction from the Lord before engaging in any battle. A seven-day march and a shout would not have won the battle at Ai (see Joshua 7 and 8) or taken out Goliath (see I Samuel 17). It was their obedience that brought down the walls of Jericho.

The requirements for successful spiritual warfare seem clear: We must be a holy people set apart for a holy cause who will obey the Lord and follow His marching orders.

A Better Way

Some strongholds are more entrenched than others. For instance, Rajneeshpuram was a squatter on the land. Even though they purchased Big Muddy Ranch, their gods were foreign to our nation, and their presence here wasn't strongly established yet. Read II

Samuel chapter 5 to understand how David's kingdom was established. Verse 12 says, "**And David realized that the LORD had established him as king over Israel, and that He had exalted his kingdom for the sake of His people Israel.**" It takes time and many battles to establish a kingdom. Rajneeshpuram was embroiled in city government issues when we just "happened" to be driving through. Additionally, prayer warriors all across the state were interceding. Our drive-through and prayers were like the final shout that brought the walls of Jericho tumbling down. Then the government stepped in and drove them from the land.

A battle is fought on multiple levels and prayer is only one of the components. Part of the strategy must include ground troops that go in and take possession of the land. Prayer and worship teams standing guard until somebody comes along and does their part to occupy the land is not a strategy—it is a half-baked plan that is destined for failure. One must follow the other in a God-orchestrated, strategically-crafted plan, or the battle will be lost, and someone will probably be hurt.

Thankfully the Lord used those years to teach us some very difficult but valuable lessons about exercising wisdom and caution instead of stepping hastily into realms where angels "fear to tread." I now believe it is possible to maximize our effectiveness as intercessors and minimize our casualties. But we did not know that in the eighties. We just barged our way in and commanded demons to flee without wisdom, strategy, or direction from the Lord.

Some will say that because of the hits and backlash intercessors and prayer warriors have experienced in the past, we should never engage in spiritual warfare. One need only look at our nation to see what happens when the church sells its birthright, relinquishes authority, and allows the enemy unchallenged entry into our nation. The church watched as the courts struck down school prayer and did little when Roe vs. Wade made abortion legal. We are again watching as foreign gods invade our land and become more entrenched each day. We cannot give up because of past losses. Instead we need to learn how to go to battle in the Lord's prescribed way and become even more strategic in warfare than our enemy. We must learn to exercise great wisdom and aim our spiritual weapons of warfare with laser-point accuracy. The remainder of this book will be devoted to understanding these principles in greater detail.

CHAPTER 4
Exodus 23 Road Map

The path of the righteous is like the first gleam of dawn, shining ever brighter till the full light of day.

(Proverbs 4:18 NLT)

Follow the Lord

In this day and age, there is no lack of information available on the topic of spiritual warfare. I have attended more conferences than I can count, read more books than I can remember, and listened to a wide assortment of anointed teaching on the subject. I have been enriched by these teachings, and I deeply respect the truths the Lord has released to the body of Christ through those who are paving the way. But there are some who would tell us all forms of spiritual warfare are wrong and dangerous. There are others who challenge principalities and powers on a daily basis without wisdom or restraint. Both of these extremes are wrong because, quite honestly, all prayer is spiritual warfare. When we praise the Lord or humble ourselves and bless the land, we are using some of the most powerful weapons of warfare available to us. Intercession is the ultimate strategy that releases God's power to accomplish things that simply will not happen unless God's people pray (see II Chronicles 7:14). Once we understand this, our prayers can move mountains, topple strongholds, and set the prisoners free.

The key to effective spiritual warfare is to follow the Lord into battle and do what He says. What may be right in one situation may be completely wrong in another. God wants His army to follow Him into battle and not follow a form or formula. According to Scripture, Jericho was defeated through six days of silence and one shout (see Joshua 6:10). In I Samuel 17:45, David challenged Goliath to his face, **"You come against me with sword and spear and javelin, but I come against you in the name of the LORD Almighty, the God of the armies of Israel, whom you have defied."** They were both successful because they did what the Lord told them to do.

The following chapters are not intended to be the final word on the subject. The Lord is revealing strategies and pieces to a large puzzle through the anointed teachings from great spiritual leaders like my pastor, Rick Joyner, and others such as Cindy Jacobs, Francis Frangipane, Dutch Sheets, Peter Wagner, and many more. Hidden treasure-troves of knowledge are available for those who are truly seeking strategies for success. Guard against narrow-thinking or a religious spirit that would try to separate us through what may appear to be differences of opinion because of the limitations of our understanding. It will take more revelation than any one person can fully understand to teach the entirety of this topic. As the Word says, we only know in part, and this book is just one very small piece to that puzzle.

These next chapters are a collection of my experiences concerning the subject, and I hope it will increase your understanding and challenge you to seek the Lord for more. Add it to your arsenal of teachings and draw upon all the resources the Lord is giving to the body of Christ in this hour. We will need it all if we are to be the army of prayer warriors the Lord is calling to action in this time.

Road Map

Paul wrote concerning the Old Testament, **"Everything that was written in the past was written to teach us" (see Romans 15:4 NIV).** In his letter to the Corinthians, he wrote that the events recorded in the Law of Moses **"happened to them as examples" (see I Corinthians 10:11 NIV).** Even though we are no longer under the Law, we can learn from the examples recorded in the Old Testament. These events have been recorded to teach us how to rule and reign in this life. The Bible is where I look for warfare strategies, how to be a watchman, and how to take and occupy the land. It is my greatest resource for information and my final authority. I encourage you to pray for discernment and keep The Bible close at hand when reading this and other books available on the subject.

Exodus 23:20–33 is my road map for taking and occupying a promised land. It will help you understand what it will take to not only rule and reign in your own land, but how to take back the Promised Land the Lord is giving to you.

> **"See, I am sending an angel ahead of you to guard you along the way and to bring you to the place I have prepared.**
> **"Pay attention to him and listen to what he says. Do not rebel against him; he will not forgive your rebellion, since my Name is in him" (Exodus 23:20-21 NIV).**

When we go to the land of our inheritance, whether it is a short-term assignment or something more, the Lord goes ahead of us and prepares the way. His angels will guard and protect us when we are following His lead. That is why it is essential we learn to discern the voice of the Lord from all the other voices in our lives. If we follow another voice, God sees it as rebellion. According to I Samuel 15:23, rebellion is the same as witchcraft and in Exodus 22:18, witchcraft was punishable by death. This is a serious offense! We probably will not be stoned when we do something the Lord has not called us to do, but we will step out from under His protective covering and become vulnerable to all the demonic forces that currently occupy the land. When the Lord is leading, He will protect us and show us the way.

> **"If you listen carefully to what he says and do all that I say, I will be an enemy to your enemies and will oppose those who oppose you.**
> **"My angel will go ahead of you and bring you into the land of the Amorites, Hittites, Perizzites, Canaanites, Hivites and Jebusites, and I will wipe them out" (Exodus 23:22-23 NIV).**

The instructions to listen are repeated because there is a lot of noise in this world, and it seems everything is shouting for our attention. It is easy to fall into traps like the cares of this world and the demands of life. We must guard our minds against distractions so we do not miss what the Lord is telling us to do. If we disregard the Lord's voice to follow the other sounds vying for our attention, He is under no obligation to oppose our enemies. We must learn to listen carefully and do all He says to do. When we follow His lead, He will be with us in battle or wherever He calls us to go. We have nothing to fear. There will be no enemy too great for us to drive out.

> **"Do not bow down before their gods or worship them or follow their practices. You must demolish them and break their sacred stones to pieces" (Exodus 23:24 NIV).**

What are the idols in your land? Are they your children, your job, entertainment, the love of money? To love anything more than the Lord is to form an ungodly attachment that can become an idol in our lives. We must be very careful not to entangle ourselves with the lifestyles and sins of the ungodly in the places to which we are called. The strongholds in our lives need to come down first, and then we can deal with the strongholds on the land the Lord is giving us.

"Worship the LORD your God"(Exodus 23:25 NIV).

We were created for worship, but true worship does not come easily to most believers. In John 4:20-24 Jesus taught that true worship was not dependent upon a location, but a Person. We read in verse 23, **"But the hour is coming, and now is, when the true worshipers will worship the Father in spirit and truth; for the Father is seeking such to worship Him."** If you are a true worshiper, it is possible to worship the Lord with all your heart in the midst of religiosity and anywhere else you happen to be. When we seek Him with all our hearts, our thirst for Him will increase, and worship will flow naturally. True worshipers drink freely from the rivers of living water. Everything else flows from that place.

> **"And his blessing will be on your food and water. "I will take away sickness from among you, and none will miscarry or be barren in your land. I will give you a full life span" (Exodus 23:25-26 NIV).**

Health, blessings, and long life are all evidence God is with us and leading us. If we are dealing with overwhelming sickness or His blessing is not visible in our lives, it is possible He is not in what we are doing. This could be a call to stand down from the battle and regroup. Spend time worshiping Him and seeking His face. Listen to what He is saying. You may need to increase your prayers and prayer covering, or you may need to withdraw altogether. Once the dust settles, find out what His strategy is for taking the land and stay within the covering and protection of His presence by staying in the Word and worshiping Him.

If you are battling demons more than you are worshiping the Lord, you are out of balance and the enemy has more of your attention than the Lord. If you have taken on a battle He has not called you to, repent, and ask Him for forgiveness. Then pray for healing and deliverance from any entanglement with the sins of the land you may have encountered.

> **"I will send my terror ahead of you and throw into confusion every nation you encounter. I will make all your enemies turn their backs and run.**
> **"I will send the hornet ahead of you to drive the Hivites, Canaanites and Hittites out of your way" (Exodus 23:27-28 NIV).**

We are the Lord's weapon against all evil, and if we are willing, He will use us to throw evil into confusion and send the enemy running. His strategy is simple: follow Him and He will put terror in the enemy as we go. He may call us to fast, sing, make a declaration, or perform some type of prophetic act. These are all part of His arsenal, and we are the carriers of His presence into battle.

> **"But I will not drive them out in a single year, because the land would become desolate and the wild animals too numerous for you.**
> **"Little by little I will drive them out before you, until you have increased enough to take possession of the land" (Exodus 23:29-30 NIV).**

When we look at all that is wrong in the world, we are tempted to want to change it all. But the truth is, if God wiped out every evil thing in a day, we would not be able to maintain it. The enemy would return seven times stronger. God's prescribed way is to deliver it into our hands a little at a time as we grow and are able to maintain and occupy the land.

Additionally, if we try to fix everything, we will only succeed at removing a little dust, but never make a real difference. Find where the Lord is leading and driving out the enemy and follow Him one step at a time.

> **"I will establish your borders from the Red Sea to the Mediterranean Sea, and from the desert to the Euphrates River" (see Exodus 23:31 NIV).**

God will give us our boundaries. We cannot be everything to everyone. Let anointed people lead where they are called to lead and let others shine at what they do. We need to stay within the boundaries the Lord has given us and focus on what we are called to do, nothing more and nothing less.

> **"I will give into your hands the people who live in the land, and you will drive them out before you.**
> **"Do not make a covenant with them or with their gods.**
> **"Do not let them live in your land or they will cause you to sin against me, because the worship of their gods will certainly be a snare to you" (see Exodus 23:31-33 NIV).**

These are strong warnings to follow every time we achieve a victory. We cannot give the land back to those who were the cause of the sins and strongholds that once reigned in the land. We cannot compromise with them because it will draw us into their lies and ultimately their sins. Once we draw a line in the sand, we dare not go back.

These are lessons the Lord taught me, and they can be applied to our Christian walk in both the natural and spiritual realms. I learned how to rule and reign in my home first, then I was given opportunities to increase my level of authority and take new ground as the Lord led me. According to the above Scriptures, there is a prescribed method for taking our promised land, little by little, until we increase enough to take possession. The next chapters are the testimony of how the Lord increased my authority and showed me how to dislodge the enemy and occupy at each level.

There are levels of spiritual warfare that require increasing levels of authority to deal with. The first step is to recognize we have authority over all that is ours, including our families, homes, ministries, and businesses. Territorial spirits are not just ruling over our cities, their influence can be found in all these places. We begin by detaching ourselves from demonic strongholds in our personal space or "garden" as I refer to in the next chapter. When we are free from these strongholds and learn to occupy with the opposite spirit, we earn the authority to set others free. If we are faithful to occupy the land that is ours, we may be called to a higher level of authority such as strategic level intercession where territorial spirits rule over geographical locations. The following chapters will demonstrate how.

Part Two

Garden Level Intercession

CHAPTER 5

Ruling and Reigning in Your Garden

"The Lord God took the man and put him in the Garden of Eden to work it and take care of it."

(Genesis 2:15 NIV)

Natural Authority versus Spirit Authority

Who has authority in your garden? A few years ago when my house was busting at the seams with my grown children, grandchildren, and their pets, I began to see my home and family as my garden. It is a beautiful five-bedroom, three-bath home with a large country kitchen, two living rooms, and a formal dining room. Way too big for me, but I had just sold my small condo in Washington, D.C. for more than double what this large house was going for, and it seemed like a great idea at the time. Tim passed away a few years before this, and

I wanted a home with room for my family when they came for visits or needed a short-term place to stay.

My granddaughter was the first to come. She has Type One Diabetes, which made the first step toward helping my family very challenging. Her parents were in a nasty custody battle at the time. Soon after she arrived, my daughter came, and eventually my son and his family needed a short-term place to stay as well. There were visits from other grandchildren, my youngest son, and his family, my parents, and my in-laws. This was a great house and a good place for people to get together, but probably not all at once. This leads me to the following discussion about our personal realms of authority.

My Garden

We all have personal space we are responsible for and have the opportunity to make better. Once the Lord has saved us and set us free from the effects of sin and death, we can look beyond ourselves to our most immediate world. That is where Adam and Eve come in. We learn from their story in Genesis 1:26 that God delegated authority to man to rule over the earth. Mankind was created to have dominion, but their sphere of authority began in the garden where Adam and Eve were tested to see if they could tend their garden and obey simple instructions. We know the story; it did not end well. But it serves to illustrate the point that God delegates a place of authority where we are expected to exercise dominion. According to Luke 19:17, we are given the opportunity to be faithful stewards in small things first. If we are faithful there, we will be given greater opportunities to exercise our authority.

For instance, because I own my home, whatever happens there is under my jurisdiction. I can paint it. I can landscape the yard. I can move furniture around. I can cook, clean (or not), and basically do whatever I want to. When I dedicated my home to the Lord, I invited Him to be the head of my household. When I invited family to move in, I delegated conditional authority to them and relinquished some of mine. I can give them permission to rearrange some of the furniture, cook meals, and take ownership in their rooms. But ultimately, I still own the house and God is in control. I can give anyone living with me some authority, but it is conditional to my rules and requirements. If they do anything that upsets me, I reserve the right to kick them out at any time, because my house is my garden, and I am responsible for it.

Even with all the people coming in and out of my home, I try to keep it clean, painted, the yard looking beautiful, and everyone inside happy. It is an endless cycle of upkeep, demands, and chores, but it is mine to do with as I please.

When Snakes Enter the Garden

In the same manner we have been delegated the authority to rule over what is ours in the natural world, we have been delegated authority in the spirit realm to rule over what belongs to us.

During the few months when my house was overrun with people, my daughter was going through a difficult divorce and fear was controlling her life. When her fear became our daily bread, the Lord woke me early one morning and told me that the boa constrictor was the family pet. I knew He was referring to the gripping, suffocating fear everyone under my roof was living with. It reminded me of the snake in the Garden of Eden.

I did a little research to understand what it would be like to have a boa constrictor as a pet. According to articles I found on the subject, having a pet boa can be overwhelming because its sheer size and presence in a home will dominate everything. An enormous enclosure (cage) is needed to accommodate a ten-foot long reptile that can weigh as much as a twelve-year-old child. I try not to imagine what it would be like to clean it. A boa will drain its owners emotionally, physically, and financially.

The feeding habits of the boa are frightening to watch. It coils its body around its prey and with each breath it will constrict, or squeeze, its coils just a little tighter until the animal can no longer breathe. Spiritually they are symbolic pictures of suffocating fear, defilement, and death to the innocent. When it gives birth, it literally multiplies itself up to forty times. If a spirit of fear is allowed to rule in the house, it will multiply in a similar manner.

I had a dream about the same time that helped me understand the gravity of our predicament. In the dream I saw a very fat man, 600 pounds or more, sitting at my table. It was a large banquet table loaded with food. The fat man had long hair. In fact, his entire body was covered with long brown hair. He reminded me of the cowardly lion from *The Wizard of Oz*. He had a crown on his head, and his eyes were covered with a bandana. I saw myself bringing a large tray of food and serving him. It was obvious he had been made king and given a place of authority at my table. I understood from the Lord that the cowardly blindfolded lion represented blinding fear. Fear had been given a place of authority at my table, and I was serving and feeding it.

Eliminating the Squatters

As good stewards of the things the Lord has given us, it is our responsibility to enforce our authority in the natural realm and in the realm of the spirit where demons can rule. If we allow them to continue to rule unchallenged in our garden, they will continue to multiply until they overtake our lives. Eliminating these demonic squatters from our garden is not difficult—it is just a matter of taking away their food and denying them a place at our tables. If we refuse to do so, we delegate our authority for them to remain.

It was obvious my daughter needed deliverance from fear. But so did the rest of us. We had all come under its control. It literally had become the family pet. We were catering to it and feeding it on a daily basis, and it was multiplying itself in each one of us. Once I recognized its stronghold in my life, I repented, broke agreement with it, and ended its control. Then I led my family in prayers of deliverance. The more people who live in your garden, the bigger this challenge is.

Once we sent the squatter away from the table and closed the door to fear, peace ruled in my garden once again.

You can follow the same steps to eliminate the unwanted demonic squatters from your home:

1. **Repent.** Ask the Lord to forgive you for allowing the unholy sprit (name the spirit) a place in your life and home.

2. **Stop feeding and serving it.** Using fear as an example, it begins by simply asking, "What if" as in, "What if I lose the kids to this horrible person? What if I go to jail? What if I lose my job?" etc. Lies are generally rooted in some degree of truth. However, there is a greater truth this lie is trying to hide. The greater truth is the Lord is in control. We are not orphans who have been abandoned to the evils of this world. Every time we agree with the lie, we are saying the Lord cannot possibly rescue us. It is like feeding the boa—the more it eats, the bigger it gets, and the more it eats. The first step toward freedom is to stop feeding the boa.

3. **Stop honoring it and bowing to its authority.** I was honoring it by giving it respect and bowing to its control.

4. **Stop allowing it to rule.** Anytime we allow demons to live unchallenged in our lives or homes we allow them the right to rule and reign.

The devil does not play fair. He will invade wherever there is an opportunity and establish his realm and demand obedience.

5. **Bind it and send it away.** Once I stopped feeding it, I did not allow fear to lay dormant and wait for another opportunity to return. I bound it according to Matthew 18:18, **"Truly I tell you, whatever you bind on earth will be bound in heaven, and whatever you loose on earth will be loosed in heaven" (NIV).** Then I sent it away from the table, out the door, and away from everything I have authority over.

6. **Close the door behind it so it will not come back.** Ask yourself, what was the open door that allowed this spirit dominion in my garden? I believed the lie that evil has more authority in my life than the Lord. We must close the door to the lie.

7. **Change your behavior.** Clean up the table, change the linens, and start over with a clean slate. The key to changed behavior is to occupy your mind and thoughts with the opposite spirit. Invite peace to rule instead of fear, and the fruit of the spirit to be in operation in your life. If it tries to come back, do not allow it to breathe the same air you are breathing! Send it away and lock the door behind it.

Prayer of Repentance and Consecration

Lord, forgive me for giving place to the spirit of (name the spirit that you are dealing with, such as fear, lust, anger, pride, etc.). I repent for agreeing with (name the spirit) and allowing it to rule over and control my life. I have given it honor, respect, and authority in my thoughts and actions and allowed it to grow unchallenged in my life and home, and for that, I am truly sorry. I have served it up like a delicious meal at my table and agreed with its lies. I have had more faith in (name the spirit) than in Your ability to deliver me. Please forgive me. From this moment on and with Your help, Lord, I will no longer bow down to this spirit or allow it to control me or my household. I refuse to give it a place in my life any longer. I will not give in to its pressure to agree with its lies and deception. And now, in the mighty name of Jesus, I renounce the spirit of (name it) and command you to leave me and my home now. I break all agreement with you. I strip you of your authority to rule in my garden, my God-given realm of responsibility, and send you to the foot of the cross where you will become the Lord's footstool. I declare that this is holy ground. The Lord rules here, and I live under His protective covering. I do not walk in darkness, but I walk in the light as He is in the Light. I put on peace, hope, love, joy, grace, forgiveness, and kindness in every area where the spirit of (name the spirit) once ruled, and I am now free! I submit myself again to You, Lord Jesus, and thank You for the privilege of walking with You in this awesome adventure. In Jesus' name and for His sake, AMEN!

Increasing Authority

Once we have established authority at the personal level, our boundaries will increase to include our neighborhoods, places of business, schools, cities, and beyond. As we are faithful to tend and watch over the places the Lord gives to us, our authority will increase. We begin by loving our neighbors as ourselves; then the Lord will give us greater authority to pray effective prayers on their behalf. Praying for our neighbor's garden is the subject of the next chapter.

Chapter 6

Praying for Someone Else's Garden

"Love the Lord your God with all your heart and with all your soul and with all your mind and with all your strength. The second is this: 'Love your neighbor as yourself.' There is no commandment greater than these."

(Mark 12:30-31 NIV)

Love First

Who has the authority in your neighbor's garden? Most of us would never dream of walking over to the divorcee's house next door and telling her, "Please pull the weeds in your garden and water your dead lawn. And, by the way, would you mind picking up the kids' toys that have been scattered all over your yard since last August?" We may not have the courage to do that, but for most people it would take even more courage to get to know her. That would require investing ourselves in a stranger's life. If you did, you might discover that her ex left her with a house she couldn't afford, three kids he never paid attention to, and huge credit card debt that she shouldn't be responsible for. Now she works two jobs, runs the kids to daycare, school, and soccer games, and has no time to water the lawn or pick up toys.

You could pray daily that she would clean up her yard, but you probably would not see any real answers to that prayer. What she needs is a friend to help shuttle her kids around and arrange a neighborhood workday to spruce up her yard. If you want to take one giant step toward enlarging your spiritual boundaries, become her friend. That is how you gain respect in her eyes and spiritual authority when praying for her garden (her home, kids, job, finances, and all that is important to her).

The same principle applies in every other area you are called to pray into. You can pray blessings, safety, health, and prosperity over the clerk at the grocery store, the mailman, or a co-worker, but to be really effective, get to know them and learn what the real needs are. You will be amazed at how much more effective your prayers are when you understand their real issues and tell them you are praying for them. Once they recognize that God is answering your prayers, they will be open to asking for prayer over their more serious issues, like a rebellious teenager or a broken marriage. You can invoke the multiplication factor by praying with them instead of for them, and the Lord will be in the midst of that prayer (see Matthew 18:19-20).

What is Conditional Authority?

When we pray for places where others have the God-given authority over what they own, our authority is conditional to theirs in the same way my family's authority was conditional to my rules when they moved into my home. We can pray for them whether they ask us or not, but our level of effectiveness will be limited. But if they ask for our prayers, or even better, agree with us in prayer, our authority will be multiplied by their agreement. On the other hand, if they contradict our prayers with fear, unbelief, and word curses, their words have the authority to sabotage our prayers.

Praying over demonic strongholds in places outside of your personal realm requires greater spiritual authority. The Lord wants us to be strong, effective prayer warriors. Until we are free from fear and all the other strongholds in our personal lives, the Lord will protect us from harm by restricting our effectiveness in areas we are not ready for. This is why our authority in other realms is not only conditional to their agreement, but it is also conditional to our spiritual maturity. Learning the lessons in our personal areas of responsibility is a prerequisite to exercising spiritual authority in other realms. When we are able to maintain and occupy what is ours in the natural and spiritual realms, the Lord will increase our ability to pray effective prayers in other realms.

The Devil Doesn't Play Fair

It is important we understand when we pray for others that we are taking on their issues and coming face-to-face with their demons. I have always prayed for the cities I lived in, local and national governments, schools, churches, and businesses, and all the people associated with these places. I believe my prayers were effective, but until I was able to deal with the demons in my home and personal life, I didn't have the authority to deal with theirs.

Here is a simple illustration. Some years ago, one of my children asked me to co-sign for a personal loan. Unknown to me was the fact that my credit rating was directly related to their ability to pay off the loan. You would think I would have known that, but Tim was usually in charge of such things. When I decided to take out a personal loan for an important purchase, I noticed my credit rating had dropped from "excellent" to "good." I was surprised because I rarely used credit and always paid my bills on time. But my child had missed a payment, and my credit rating dropped. Amazingly unfair isn't it? That is the principle in operation when we decide to rescue people from the enemy's lies and traps. Let me explain:

When we minister to someone who is steeped in

shame and bitterness, and we have self-pity and rejection issues ourselves, it will not be long before we are drinking from the same bitter cup they are drinking from. Their sins can affect us in the same way my child's credit rating affected me. It may not be fair, but it is a fact of life.

What is the answer to such a dilemma? Break agreement with the enemy, get delivered, and get set free first! Tell the devil your account has been paid in full by the blood of Jesus—he can no longer demand payment. A clean slate is the only answer, and Jesus is the only solution. If we are not tending our own gardens, in all likelihood, snakes in the form of demonic spirits will fill that void. The same is true of the people we are praying for. Once we are free, we will have greater authority to plead the blood over others and set them free from the traps and lies of the enemy.

Jesus addressed this situation in John 14:30, **"I will not say much more to you, for the prince of this world is coming. He has no hold over me" (NIV).** Jesus is the only one who was completely free from the enemy's hold. He is our example of the Perfect Intercessor. His prayers were heard, and everyone He touched was set free because the devil had nothing on Him. We are all in the process of deliverance, and our authority is increasing with every breakthrough. The answer to freedom for all the captives is Christ in us, the hope of glory (see Colossians 1:27). He paid our debt in full, and the devil has no recourse against that.

Marketplace Intercession

I lived in Washington, D.C. for four years after my husband passed away. During that time, Jeff Ahern, a friend and the leader of the life group I attended, asked me to be a part of his new business. The Lord had given him a vision for marketplace intercession for business leaders. Thanks to visionaries like Lance Wallnau, this new concept was starting to be recognized in Christian business owner's circles. In this role, I had the privilege of counseling and interceding for a wide variety of business owners such as building contractors, electrical engineers, IT companies, manufacturers, political candidates, and more. In the process, I have learned a great deal about praying with authority in someone else's garden.

Jeff and I have found that our most effective prayers in the business world occur when the owners are involved in the process. We have seen small businesses that were barely making it transformed into multi-million dollar companies with this simple approach. Not all are changed that dramatically, but in every case there has been a major impact on their lives and their businesses. What starts out as a small local company will often expand, and in some cases, even open new branches in other states. Some are getting ready to launch their business in other nations. One company has done so well they are planning an exit strategy in the near future and getting more involved in politics, their real passion. Many have their own ministries in addition to their businesses and are able to finance greater works and mission projects now that business is improving. It is also satisfying to see owners finally understand their true calling and purpose in life and get better at what they do as a result of intercession.

Several years ago we were called upon to intercede for a small manufacturing company in Milford, Delaware. At the time, First State Manufacturing was barely able to stay afloat. Sher Valenzuela, the Vice President, described their situation in a testimony she wrote for our website:

> "When our company began working with SOZO Services in the Fall of 2008, we could truly relate to the 'crushed on every side' referenced in II Corinthians 4:8. Debilitating issues abounded, ranging from cash flow bottlenecks to owners struck by illness. Non-stop distractions constantly kept us from being able to effectively deal with what we needed to do to keep our doors open. 'Rogue' employees actively worked to cause us harm, and baseless accusations forced time-consuming responses to satisfy bureaucratic requirements. No matter how hard we worked, it never seemed to be enough. Finally, and not a moment too soon, it became evident we needed something more.
>
> "Were I to timeline the power of our partnership, it would quickly become evident. It wasn't like our business experienced a sudden launch . . . the truth is at that time we might have been too weak to hang on if it had! But what became apparent was that

> our business began to 'hum.' Personnel issues settled, the right people took their post, production and sales pipelines opened, favor was found, and we ended up having a record-setting year in a multitude of ways. Simply put, when we became 'grafted in' with SOZO Services, our issues became their issues, our breakthroughs became their breakthroughs, and the forces of hell could not prevail."

The turnaround in their business could have been attributed to a lot of things. There are skeptics who would say they were on the verge of success anyway and it was just a matter of timing. But the truth is they had been a small company for nearly fifteen years, barely keeping their staff employed and paying their bills. When we began dealing with the demonic strongholds in the company, the enemy's traps were broken and his plans for their demise were spoiled. As Sher said, their company began to "hum."

Our partnership with an IT company began in a similar way. They were barely keeping up with their bills, struggling with employee issues, customer complaints, and personal problems. We focused on their personal issues first, and then the employee problems began to settle down as new hires with more dedication and experience took their places. Finally, sales started to increase, and now they are looking for a larger facility. They have made connections overseas and are getting ready to make the jump to light speed with single contracts that are larger than their average yearly income.

Another company was referred to us and gave our team a test run to see if having intercessors would make a difference. After the test run, our new friends decided to keep us. They are beginning to open branches in new locations and work on future projects overseas. They are lovely people and dear friends. That is what I enjoy the most with this approach to prayer. We become a part of their team, or more accurately, a part of their family. Our intercession is effective because they trust us, agree with our prayers, and give us the authority to call things into order in their garden.

Another business is a re-seller for a well-known copier company. They were dealing with many of the same issues—cash flow problems, employee issues, low sales, and their family was experiencing debilitating health issues. To complicate matters, they seemed to be experiencing demonic manifestations in their home and office. They decided to see if "paying for prayer" really worked. That is a misnomer, and sadly, an idea most people have trouble getting past. Jeff corrects that misleading terminology by simply saying, "People pay us for our time; the prayer is free." I like that.

We were able to help them bless and not curse their business and to praise the Lord instead of blaming the devil for all of their problems. The culture in their office began to change and we have seen a turnaround in their health issues, their financial issues are beginning to be resolved, and employee issues are going away. A visit to their site opened opportunities to shift things in the spirit realm and rid them of the unwanted demonic activity.

The Lord gives us a different strategy for each business. I will often write a prayer for their situation and either go to their site and pray it with them, or when that is not possible, give them the strategy for reclaiming their business. We always involve the business owners in the process. I wrote the following prayer aimed at reclaiming a business from the strongholds of the enemy. I recommended the declarations be spoken at the start of the reclaiming prayer walk and that they take Communion at the end. We titled it, *A Blessing for Kingdom Advancement.* Since then it has been rewritten many times for various groups, but this is the essence of the prayer.

A Blessing for Kingdom Advancement

We bless (name of business or ministry) in the name of the Lord Jesus Christ, who is our stronghold, our strength, and our salvation. This is our appointed time to advance our kingdom purposes on the earth. As God's faithful stewards, we are recipients of all the blessings, favor, grace, and honor due to (name of business or ministry) to advance this cause. We declare that all things that have been stored up for us and everything that rightfully belongs to us are being released into our hands.

We bless our staff, employees, families, clients, vendors, and associates to be safe under the Lord's covering. We stand on the Word of the Living God that says no weapon formed against us shall prosper. We repent and break agreement with fear, doubt, unbelief, and failure. We stand on the Word of God that says the same Spirit that raised Christ from the dead dwells in us! We put on kingdom authority, clothe ourselves with the full armor of God, take up the weapons of warfare, and go to war and defend what is rightfully ours.

We put a halt to all plots and plans of the enemy to take us off course, meddle with our heritage, or cause harm to our business, family, employees, associates, and clients. We build a hedge of protection and draw a bloodline around this business. We deny the enemy access to all who gather here, and we command that demonic interruptions in our affairs cease now. We rest in the safety and protection of our Lord and Savior, Jesus Christ. The blood of Jesus covers us. We are hidden from the enemy's lies, schemes, and tactics.

We declare we are free from all debt, sickness, and bondage that have come upon us through the kingdom of darkness. We stop every weapon and trap set for us and put a halt to all witchcraft prayers, spells, curses, and harsh, critical words spoken against this business, staff, employees, associates, family, and friends. We reverse the curse of witchcraft and controlling words and decree that they will not stand, take root, or come to pass.

From this day forward, we operate according to God's timetable. God's agenda is our agenda. Our ears and eyes are in tune to heaven's frequency. What God is doing in this hour, we are doing. What He is saying in this hour, we are saying. Our set time will not be frustrated. We will not suffer shame. Our mountain will not be surrendered.

(Name of business or ministry) is built with a precious cornerstone and a sure foundation whose walls are not made with human hands but whose architect and builder is God. These are sacred grounds with a holy cause and purpose. Poverty, debt, failure, fear, doubt, sickness, and disease, are no longer in operation here. Blessings, favor, and every good thing abound. Divine boundaries and borders are established and the laws of the kingdom of heaven now govern all actives here. In the mighty name of Jesus, our Lord and Savior, AMEN!

Praying for Marriages

When we intercede for a business, we pray fervently for families and especially marriages. Business owners often put eighty or more hours a week into their company and see very little of their spouses. Their entire world revolves around employee issues, cash flow worries, legal problems, and the stress of meeting payroll each month. This can be a disaster in the making for their personal lives. We have learned that no matter how awesome our prayers for them may be, unless they learn to seek the Lord first in their business and their family, the problems will not go away. So we teach them how to run a kingdom business, pour Scriptures into them, and we teach them how to pray.

I like writing prayers, especially for husbands and wives who do not know how to pray for each other. Like a doctor writing a prescription, I will write a blessing and tell them to pray it daily over each other until they begin to experience change.

The following blessing for a husband is meant to be prayed by his wife:

A Blessing for Husbands

I bless you in the name of Jesus to be a man after God's heart, a worshiper of God, living daily in His presence, walking in His ways, and passionate about His desires. I bless you with the wisdom of Solomon, to understand the deep things of God, to excel in your business, and to prosper in all you do. I bless you to be like Joseph, the faithful servant who became a prince of Egypt.

I bless you to make wise decisions, to deal with business matters intelligently, and to manage your affairs with integrity. I bless you with generosity and kindness, to not be jealous or keep a record of wrongs, but to always hope for the best when things are at their worst and to see the good in people more than their faults. I bless you to be a humble and faithful steward of the gifts God has given you and to increase in your anointing as you shepherd those entrusted to your care.

I bless you to judge rightly and fairly and to cause others to prosper by your wise counsel. I bless you to be the head of your household and a husband who loves his wife like Christ loves the church. I bless you with spiritual authority over your home to defend the ground that is yours. I bless your words to be sharp, powerful, and full of faith to defend all God has given you against the wiles of the devil.

I bless you to walk in truth and righteousness, to be a man whose thoughts are under the control of the Holy

Spirit and who speaks the oracles of God. I bless you with an anointed tongue so what you proclaim in the heavenlies will call into order things on earth. Your prayers will right wrongs, bring healing, set captives free, and deliver the oppressed.

I bless you to go forth in the power of the Holy Spirit to take dominion over all the territory the Lord has given you. I bless you to prosper in everything you put your hand to, knowing it is by His grace and anointing, and not your own. I bless you to receive every resource you need that pertains to godliness and righteousness for the purpose of establishing His covenant and His kingdom here on earth.

I bless you to be a man of faith, courage, and confidence, who walks humbly before God, knowing who you are in Christ. You are valuable, highly esteemed, and favored in the kingdom of God, skilled, anointed, and sought after by the kingdoms of the earth.

I bless you to grow in confident assurance that God is at work perfecting you to be all these things and more. In the name of Jesus our Lord and Savior, AMEN.

The next prayer is for husbands to pray over their wives.

A Blessing for Wives

I bless you in the name of Jesus, to be a woman of God, highly esteemed, full of grace, noble, strong, and courageous.

I bless you to live a long and healthy life, fulfilling your highest calling for your time on earth. You are blessed to be active and productive all the days of your life, full of good works, and a life well lived.

I bless you to be an encouragement and inspiration to all who come your way, to shine brightly across all denominations, cultures, and groups, and to freely bless others with the gifts the Lord has given you. I bless you with an increasing anointing to the proportion that you steward what God has already given you.

I bless you to be seen for who you are, a woman of faith, with purpose and destiny, a world changer, a visionary, an example for others to follow, a lover of God, a lover of your husband and family, and gifted to be a blessing wherever the Lord leads you.

I bless you with the ability to learn new things, accept challenges, see hope when things seem hopeless, to believe for the best when things are at their worst, to see the good in people and to call things that are not as though they were.

I bless you with spiritual authority, to not be shaken by the world systems or the enemy's lies, but to rise up in confidence and take the land God is giving you.

I bless you to walk confidently as a child of the King and an ambassador on earth to advance His cause.

I bless you to fear God and not man and to believe that what He began in you He will carry on to completion. You are a Proverbs 31 woman, an Esther, a Mary, an Abigail, a Rebecca all wrapped into one, a favored daughter of God and a blessing to all who meet you. In the mighty name of Jesus, AMEN.

Next Steps

Once you have learned to intercede effectively for others, the Lord may call you to step into a higher level of spiritual warfare called strategic level intercession, where principalities, powers, and rulers in high places hold entire cities and nations captive. Not everyone is called to pray at this level, but it is important that you have some understanding to know if you have a part to play. The next chapter will shed more light on this.

Part Three

Strategic Level Intercession

Chapter 7
Strategic Level Intercession

"I will send my terror ahead of you and throw into confusion every nation you encounter. I will make all your enemies turn their backs and run.

"I will send the hornet ahead of you to drive the Hivites, Canaanites and Hittites out of your way."

(Exodus 23:27-28)

Casualties of War

My husband was a spiritual gladiator. We prayed for over twenty years to be relocated to Washington, D.C. Our hearts had long been burdened with the desire to setup a 24/7 prayer covering in the heart of our nation's capital. He was hired by the Bureau of Land Management to be the National Soils Leader, and we moved to D.C. with great plans and a sense of excitement. Tim's office was within a few blocks of the White House, and he spent his daily lunch hour eating a sack lunch in Lafayette Square and praying for the President. We did not know it then, but Tim was already in the advanced stages of brain cancer. It was only a short nine months later that he died. He was precious seed to the Lord.

The interesting thing about Tim is that the world had no real attachment to him. He lived his life to be with Jesus. He was ready to die at any moment just to walk the golden streets of heaven. His brother and father were already there, and he looked forward to joining them someday. So even though I fought for his life in prayer and countless others interceded on his behalf, heaven's hold on him was stronger. He gladly laid down his life as one of the gladiators in the Lord's army even though at the time, such a thought never occurred to him.

When he died, it seemed as though my life ended and began at the same time. I was able to stand on his shoulders and move beyond his ceiling. Had he not followed the call to move to Washington, D.C., I would still be in Colorado or somewhere on the West Coast where most of my family lives. But because he blazed the trail to Washington, I was able to start a ministry there and do all the things I had learned while living in much smaller cities. What I had seen on a small scale could be applied to any location. Only this time, I came with a treasure trove of valuable lessons learned the hard way. It appeared the Lord had given me a second chance.

John Paul Jackson wrote a timely book called *Needless*

Casualties of War that has helped shed much needed light on the subject of strategic level intercession. When spiritual warfare was becoming popular in the 1980s, many intercessors were engaging in strategic level prayer with little training or understanding. This was new ground, and those of us who were diving into this arena were pioneers who thought dealing with principalities and powers in high places would be easy. The Lord was calling us to take back what the enemy had stolen, and people were beginning to learn about combat at the highest levels. Unfortunately, we were an undisciplined army without a plan or a strategy. Consequently, those who were praying against territorial spirits suffered unforeseen attacks and casualties resulted. However, not all of these casualties were needless. Their mistakes became the bedding soil for this next generation of intercessors to reap a precious harvest. They are the ones who will benefit from the lessons learned the hard way and wisdom gained from failure. Now doors of understanding are beginning to open that were like brass to our predecessors. It is a wondrous time to be in the Lord's army.

The Real Battleground

Like it or not, we are in a battle. We have been in this war since the day we were conceived, and it will continue until the day we die. Scripture tells us in Ephesians 6:12, **"For we do not wrestle against flesh and blood, but against principalities, against powers, against the rulers of the darkness of this age, against spiritual hosts of wickedness**

in the heavenly places" (NKJV). The battle is not against our unbelieving boss, or our pagan neighbor; it is against the demonic realm. If we are alive, we will bump up against their strongholds on a daily basis. Just blessing our city or praying for our neighborhood will anger territorial spirits. Writing a blog with an opinion about your local school is drawing a line in the sand and announcing to the spirit realm that you disagree with their agenda. We need to get over whatever it is in our heads that says we cannot tear down strongholds. We are chipping away at them daily without even knowing it. However, directly opposing principalities without the Lord's command or strategy will leave us open to a counter attack.

I have dear friends who went to war and sacrificed everything to lead the charge on their home ground. Some fell out of favor with their home churches and local ministries, or became a burden because their health deteriorated during the long days and nights of praying for our nation and its leaders. These trailblazers used the tools they had and laid the foundation. I believe this next generation of intercessors can learn from them. We have an opportunity to build upon these stones that have already been laid and move beyond their limitations. I pray this chapter will help those of you who are called to a higher level of spiritual warfare learn how to go to battle in the Lord's prescribed way, maximizing your effectiveness and minimizing your casualties.

Lessons Learned

Not all intercessors are called to wage warfare at the strategic level where principalities, powers, and rulers enforce their evil agenda from high places. I have seen marriages come under attack, families fall apart, and churches split when intercessors take on geographical strongholds and territorial spirits that they are not equipped to handle. The following paragraphs are the lessons I have learned over the years that may help you discern what battles you are called to and how to prepare to be an effective intercessor without bringing harm to yourself or others.

Get your assignments from the Lord. Before entering into any battle, ask the Lord if this is your assignment. No one can tell you what your prayer assignment is, so be careful that you do not go running after every opportunity that comes your way. There are great intercession ministries doing awesome things and making bold advances for the kingdom. If you sense you are called to join them, go in confidence. If you are not being called by the Lord to join their battle, do not feel condemned—trust the Lord to direct you. Remember, He will protect you from entering into a battle you are not called to. Seek counsel from others you trust if you are not sure.

Stay on target. Most intercessors have antennas pulling in information from the spirit realm and will sense demonic activity coming from various people and places. When they come into an unfamiliar territory, they can tell by the gift of discernment what spirits are dominant or active there. While this is a wonderful gift, it can be debilitating if they allow their sensitivity to pull them into alignment with these spirits. Spirits of oppression or infirmity that rule the land can take an intercessor completely out of the battle if they receive the symptoms.

Learn to pull down your antennas and focus on the Lord's assignment. Do not get pulled into someone else's battle. When you begin to sense or hear things in the spirit realm, take note, but do not engage or connect to it. Not everything you sense or hear is a calling card to engage in the battle. In the same way that your natural senses can see, hear, and touch the world in which we live, your spiritual senses can see a broad spectrum in the realm of the spirit. We must learn to focus our attention where our attention is due and allow the rest to stay on the canvas before us. The Lord is painting a picture for us to understand the spirit realm in a geographical location as a whole. But He will not give us an assignment that we are not fully prepared for. Jesus was touched by the feeling of our infirmities. He understood our physical and emotional needs because He felt them, but He did not allow those feelings to overcome Him, and neither should we.

Get your spouse's blessing. I have seen marriages come under attack and children get caught in the throes of war when intercessors jumped into a battle without the blessing and prayer covering of their spouses. Does this mean if you have an unbelieving spouse you can never be involved in strategic level intercession? That is a question I cannot answer for you. I can only tell you what I have seen and experienced. Our family was very strong in our relationship with the Lord and our commitment to prayer, and yet we lost many battles. As you know, this has not stopped me, rather it has served to teach me greater wisdom and instill a strong desire to choose my battles carefully because I do not want to bring harm to those who are dear to me. The battles will not go away, but if you allow the Lord to lead and teach you, He will use every loss to further your understanding and effectiveness as an intercessor.

If you go toe-to-toe with a demonic stronghold or territorial spirits, keep in mind that you bring your entire family with you, because they will become a target. Wherever there is a crack in the armor or a weakness in the flesh, the enemy will target it to take you out of the battle. Our children were targets for years, and it sidelined us during that time. In the process, however, we learned to measure our steps and chose our battles with more wisdom. We grew stronger as worshipers of the Lord and less like warriors. This was the Lord's intended purpose so we would learn the correct posture for any level of intercession.

Do not be a lone ranger. Be a team player—lone rangers are easy marks for the enemy. Submit yourselves to a pastoral covering. Pastors are there to protect the sheep from harm. If you are in a church that does not understand your role as an intercessor, it is still important that your spiritual leaders know your calling and pray for you. One of the most valuable lessons I learned over the years is that everyone who is on the front lines of battle needs a strong prayer covering. If your church does not want you involved in strategic level intercession, you should not engage in it.

On my first prayer walk around the Supreme Court in Washington, D.C., I was immediately aware of the demonic ruler standing guard over it. I prayed silently in the spirit as I walked all around the building. As usual there were many people standing around, including the ever present team of silent prayer warriors who stand on behalf of the unborn. About halfway around the building, I saw the ruling spirit over the Supreme Court turn directly toward me. Up until that moment I had been able to live in D.C. undetected by the principalities guarding the city. Something changed that day, and I knew I was being engaged by a new enemy.

At the time, I was the pastor's assistant in the one church in D.C. that had an understanding of such things, and I was on an assignment for them. The pastors asked me to begin leading a prayer team to pray over D.C. When I returned that day, I told them I needed at least five of the strongest prayer warriors in the city to cover our team daily. We put together the list of five. I put our names and something about each one of us on a laminated bookmark to keep in their Bibles to remind them to pray, and I made it a point to contact them weekly for updates and prayer requests. Additionally, I asked each member of our team to build up their own prayer support, keeping them informed and having them pray daily. We also prayed for each other regularly and prayed a protective covering over our families before and after each prayer walk.

Be Set Apart. "Consecrate yourselves for tomorrow the Lord will do amazing things among you" (Joshua 3:5 NIV). Just before the Israelites crossed over into the Promised Land to take Jericho, Joshua went through the camp giving orders to the people to be set apart and holy. The Lord was getting ready to deliver the Promised Land into their hands, and these were the requirements to receive the promise. To be safe on the battlefield, the Lord is calling us to be free from demonic attachments and set apart for His purposes. We are entering into such a season, and the Lord is calling His bride to be spotless for this purpose. It is time to sanctify ourselves and be ready to take the land He is preparing to deliver into our hands.

The Power of Blessing

During my assignment in Washington, my pastors asked us to refrain from engaging the enemy and instead to focus our intercession on blessing the city and government agencies centered there. That may sound like a powerless and pointless assignment, but it did not take long to understand the wisdom behind it. When visiting intercessors came to town, they often came to pray against one or more of the massive strongholds in the area and then leave. They did not understand the most basic elements in effective spiritual warfare, such as knowing if this was the Lord's assignment or theirs, connecting and working with the local people in authority, and having a plan in place to occupy the ground once they left. They missed the resulting backlash, but we did not.

Our team prayer walked around the White House each week. We spoke life over everything, blessed the people, declared Scriptures, and sang songs of deliverance. The team remained faithful to that watch until the end of George W. Bush's term in office.

One night while on this assignment, I dreamed I was President Bush's secretary. Someone came and captured me, stuffed me into a sleeping bag, spray painted my face a bright red, and dragged me outside. The sleeping bag was tight enough to keep my hands and feet bound. The next thing I knew I was being planted in a sand dune overlooking the Chesapeake Bay, facing an enormous warship. The ship was decked out with huge war guns and every one was pointed directly at me. I turned and looked back at the White House, and I could see President Bush writing at his desk. I realized that, as his intercessor, I had become the target of every attack intended for him. This opened my eyes to the sobering fact of what it really means to be an intercessor. When we stand in the gap on behalf of someone else, we protect them, and in turn, we become the target. That is why we must be rightly aligned with the Lord and His Word, walk in holiness, and stay saturated and covered in prayer! If I had tried to engage the warship in battle, I doubt I would have survived. But I had a different assignment, to bless and not curse, to build up and not pull down. There were times the Lord sent in His generals and greater battles took place, but for this assignment and our small prayer team, we stayed the course and honored the guidelines set by our pastors. I believe the President was protected from much more than we could have possibly known during that time.

We stood guard over the Capitol and had opportunities to pray on the House and Senate floors before important votes. There were occasions to pray with Congressmen and Senators and their staffs. Once we dropped into one of the well-known Senator's offices without an appointment and asked if we could pray with him. He was at a press conference at the time, so we prayed with one of his young staffers. The prayer team asked this staffer how we could pray for her, and she told us the Senator was very old, and he was worried that he had not been able to do everything he wanted to do before he passes on. We prayed for her and the Senator. She was crying tears of gratitude when we left. We stepped outside and watched the Senator engaging with the media, and I was overwhelmed by the Lord's love for this man. He was so frail-looking in person. He looked much more daunting on camera. He was just a man doing what he felt the Lord had called him to do. I realized my differences with him had kept me from praying for him, and I determined to no longer just pray with those I agreed with. I believe a stronghold in my life came down that day, and the Lord moved in the Senator's life. It was not long before he died from brain cancer, but I believe he fulfilled his purpose on this earth.

You may wonder if our time in D.C. really accomplished anything. The elections in 2008 were a tremendous disappointment for many. While we were standing guard in D.C., there were countless others doing the same thing from their homes, churches, places of business, and ministries all across our nation. Apostles, prophets, pastors, prayer generals, and their teams came to Washington frequently, fervent prayers were prayed, and people wept and cried out to the Lord.

I looked at my prayer journal to see what I had written on Election Day. I found a copy of an email I had written to a friend in my notes for that day.

> *"All is not lost. I feel the Lord smiling and saying, remember My resurrection. I believe this will be a season when we will see His resurrection power in the midst of seemingly hopeless situations. God loves people, and even though we don't deserve His mercy and grace, I believe it delights Him to pour it out anyway. I just want to say, don't lose hope. God hasn't forgotten us! We are on His mind constantly, and He is willing us to win. Even though this looks like the final inning, we could go into overtime! Remember the Angels and Red Sox!"*

I had to Google the overtime game between the Angels and Red Sox that year because I did not remember anything about it. My friend is a big Red Sox fan and I half remember him asking me if I was watching the game that night, so I decided to turn it on. I am sure it was the only game I watched the entire season, and I cannot remember watching another game since then. This is what I came across on the ESPN website:

ESPN MLB, 7:27 PM ET, October 5, Fenway Park, Boston, Massachusetts

BOSTON – After 11 consecutive losses and two straight playoff sweeps, the Los Angeles Angels had grown tired of being a bump in Boston's road to the World Series.

"I don't ever want to hear about that streak again. Ever. It's over," center fielder Torii Hunter said Sunday night after the Angels beat the Red Sox 5-4 in 12 innings to force their first-round AL playoff series to a fourth game. "We were trying to get that first win out of the way and then you could see the smiles on people's faces when we got in here."

God is willing us to win! Prayers are never wasted. They are what make it possible to go into overtime. The Lord will give us as many innings as we need to score the winning point. Remember the resurrection. The enemy thought he had won the game, but in the last inning, Jesus rose from the grave and conquered death and hell. He scored the winning point! We are not just a bump on the enemy's road to success. We have resurrection power dwelling in us, and the only way we can lose is if we give up before the game is over.

Will we ever truly be effective at turning our nation back to God if we ignore the strongholds holding our nation and those we love in captivity? Imagine if the Israelites had given up after their failure at Ai (see Joshua 7). The Promised Land might still be in the hands of the Amorites, Hittites, Perizzites, Canaanites, and all the other "ites."

Our nation is at the crossroad where right and wrong have been twisted and religious freedom and biblical values are hanging in the balance. Christians with a biblical worldview are recognizing the serious moral and spiritual decay overtaking our land. The good news is, according to II Chronicles 7:14, we can make a difference through prayer. In the next chapter, I will tell you how to line up the dominoes and start a chain reaction in your state.

CHAPTER 8

Interceding for Your Cities and States

"But you will receive power when the Holy Spirit comes on you; and you will be my witnesses in Jerusalem, and in all Judea and Samaria, and to the ends of the earth."

(Acts 1:8 NIV)

The Real Adventure

As a child growing up in southern California, I always loved visiting Disneyland. Adventureland, Fantasyland, Tomorrowland, and all the other lands ignited my imagination, and I began to see the world as one giant theme park. Just as Disneyland is full of exciting experiences, flying cannonballs, waterfalls, pirates, and castles, our lives can be a great adventure.

Our time on earth is brief. One day we will be in our heavenly home, but until then, we have an invitation to do mighty exploits for the Lord. Instead of complaining about all the darkness and evil in the world, I look at it as the adventure of a lifetime. I am called to rule and reign in this life. Aren't you?

Like ancient Israel, we are called to take our promised land. I have noticed that some believers are content to live in Fantasyland, partaking of the blessings and joys of the abundant life, but never fully aware of the battle raging all around them. Others live in Tomorrowland always looking to the future for the day when we all get to heaven, and never seeing the needs surrounding them today. Unknown to most Christians is that it is all an illusion. If we were to go behind the scenes and look at the structures keeping the park together, we would see it is just a façade held in place with wooden frames, paint, and cement. The real adventure is just outside the walls of our comfort zones.

Teamwork

Strategic level intercession for cities or states is not all that dissimilar from other levels of spiritual warfare. It is just bigger and will take a lot more people and time. This can be a great adventure. If God has called you to such an exploit, one of the greatest challenges will be how to work with the army the Lord will be amassing. We may live in Adventureland, but if we are going to understand the issues in Tomorrowland or any other land in our vicinity, we will need to connect with the believers and intercessors whose lives are invested there.

Two important fundamentals must always be remembered if the Lord is calling you to do mighty exploits for Him in your cities and states. Lone rangers are an easy target for the enemy, and the enemy will always try to fracture a team. Gathering people together for the battle is fraught with challenges, but it is necessary. The Lord has order and discipline for His army. There are generals, privates, and everything in between, and we need them all.

It will take a great deal of humility to work with people who come from different churches and spiritual backgrounds. As I wrote in the first chapter, we all have a different DNA. The minute we begin to believe we know more, or that our training and experiences have greater value than the rest of the team, we will undermine the group and stir up jealousy, competitiveness, backbiting, and more. On the other hand, if we stick with only the people we agree with, we will probably stay in Adventureland and forfeit all the other lands we may be called to help liberate. It took the entire nation of Israel, all twelve tribes, to take possession of the Promised Land. They fought together, taking cities and dying for each other as they advanced. It will not be easy, but it is the Lord's prescribed way.

How to Change a City

During our tenure in Oregon, the Lord told us that the key to revival in our community was unity. Not merely unity within our own church, but with all the church denominations in the area. So we devoted several years to getting to know the churches, their congregations, and their unique doctrines. We got to know the Baptists, Lutherans, Pentecostals, Episcopalians, Methodists, and Charismatics. It was quite an experience and worth the effort. When we put on concerts of prayer, hosted prayer breakfasts, and called for corporate early morning prayer watches, people came. Prayer was always at the center of everything we did. During that time of pressing in together for our communities, a youth center opened on Main Street as a place for kids to hang out and learn more about the Lord. Churches started to thrive and grow in the cities to the east and west of us. The local Christian radio station offered a continuous flow of praise over the valley that helped unite everyone.

While praying for our community, the Lord gave me a vision of a blackbird without any eyes circling the entire valley. In the center of this setting was a tall imposing witch who directed the path of the blackbird. I understood from the vision that a witchcraft spirit was controlling the entire area through spiritual blindness. I felt compelled to pray for the whole valley. With Bible in hand and great faith, I called the entire land my inheritance and began to reclaim it from the blindness holding it captive.

In a time when Christians kept to themselves, stayed out of politics, turned a blind eye to the advancement of secularism in the schools, and were completely oblivious to the devil's schemes, eyes were beginning to open. When it was discovered that the new video store was renting pornography, a unified band of believers requested the storeowners remove it—and they did. When politicians came to town who favored abortion, they were met with a group of picketers. When school boards met to discuss new curriculum, concerned citizens started showing up. It was a quiet uprising, but people were beginning to see the devil was having more impact on their community than the Lord, and they decided to do something about it.

Boundaries and Prayer Walks

Genesis 13:14-17 was my simple strategy and the basis for prayer walking my city and calling others to do the same. In the early eighties, I had never heard anyone use this term before, but it seemed natural to call it a "prayer walk." Later I learned the Lord was calling people everywhere to this type of intercession for their cities.

> **The Lord said to Abram after Lot had parted from him, "Look around from where you are, to the north and south, to the east and west.**
> **All the land that you see I will give to you and your offspring forever.**
> **I will make your offspring like the dust of the earth, so that if anyone could count the dust, then your offspring could be counted.**
> **Go, walk through the length and breadth of the land, for I am giving it to you" (Genesis 13:14-17 NIV).**

The public schools in the area were a big focus at the time because of the troubling trend toward secular humanism and the impact it was having on our children. I pulled together a growing number of prayer warriors, and we walked and prayed around the high school faithfully for several weeks. When we felt it was time, we read the Scripture from Joshua 6:16, **"Shout! For the Lord has given you the city!" (NIV)** and followed with a big shout and a blast from my husband's trumpet. Later our kids told us one of the teachers had a Buddha statue on his desk. For some reason, he decided to put it in his closet during the time we were praying around the school. We prayed at night so we knew he did not do this for our sake. The night we gave the shout and trumpet blast, the Buddha in his closet crashed to the floor.

When the wall collapses, charge straight in! (see Joshua 6:20)

Shortly after this, the Lord led us to start a monthly youth prayer breakfast for the public high school. We rented a hall and pulled together a few willing volunteers, musicians, and speakers. We cooked a hearty breakfast and invited all the high school kids to come and join us. As amazing as it sounds, we literally packed the place out. Most of the kids did not go to church or know the Lord as their personal Savior, but they came to see what all the commotion was about.

At the first breakfast, I was supposed to lead a few songs before the speaker gave his testimony. I knew if this was going to be successful, we needed all the kids to stand up and participate. Otherwise, they would have remained seated and made all the other kids uncomfortable, and the whole thing would have been a failure. Before we started, I asked our team to pray we could accomplish this impossible feat. When it came time, I said, "On the count of three, I want everyone in the room to stand up." I smiled outwardly, but on the inside I was holding my breath. By the time I said, "Three!" they all jumped to their feet, and we had a rousing thirty minutes of singing followed by an amazing testimony from our guest speaker.

Local Christian musicians came to play and sing for us. Once we invited a Christian school from the West Coast to come and perform skits and share their testimonies. During a breakfast in October, a few days before Halloween, my husband shared his remarkable testimony followed by a skit the Christian kids in the group did to Carmen's "The Champion" album. The students were so impacted they invited us to do the skit again for the high school music department concert. Remember this was a secular high school and not a Christian school. Their teacher approved, and on the night of the concert, our team acted out the battle of the ages between light and darkness, Jesus and Satan, in front of all the students and their parents to strobe lights and the sounds of "The Champion." It was a rousing success!

During this time the school board president was replaced by a Spirit-filled Christian believer, and a Christian principal was hired at the middle school.

The last year we were there, our son was elected student body president. He was one who never held back his faith and led many to the Lord. These were some of the indications that the enemy's stronghold was being shaken. Many of the kids who came to these prayer breakfasts were saved, set free, and delivered and continue to serve the Lord today.

Delaware is Beginning to Shake!

Years later, the Lord connected my business partner, Jeff, and I to the people of Delaware through business intercession. What started out with one business client paved the way for us to intercede for many business owners who, like most of us, were also involved in their churches and communities, loved their neighbors, and wanted the best for their cities and state. We have had the opportunity to pray for all of these areas, and in the process, doors have opened to reclaim Delaware for the Lord's true intended purposes. Marketplace and government leaders, ministries, churches, pastors, apostles, prophets, and others have contacted us to help train intercessors and put together a strategy uniting a vision to change the entire state.

Delaware was one of the original thirteen colonies. In 1787, the state became the first to ratify the Constitution of the United States and became known as The First State. Residents take great pride in this title and are unified in this one belief, as The First State goes, so goes the nation.

Delaware is located in the mid-Atlantic region and is the second smallest state in the United States. It is divided into three counties, New Castle to the north, Sussex to the south, and Kent is in the center of the state. New Castle County is more industrialized while the two lower counties are predominately agricultural. New Castle County is also the center of the state's population, and the most liberal. According to "Parenting Magazine", Wilmington, Delaware's largest city is the most dangerous small city in the nation. It is located in New Castle County. Registered voters in this county carry the state to the far left in politics and is an ongoing focus of much prayer.

Without good people responding and making changes at every level of culture and influence in the state, answers to prayer will be short-lived. God has given us leaders of influence in all three counties who are already making inroads in their communities. They are hungry enough for change to go to war for what is rightfully theirs. These are the movers and shakers who are ready, willing, and able to occupy what the Lord is delivering into their hands through prayer and intercession.

As of this writing, and even before this book is finished, a strategic plan to train intercessors, support prayer teams, and unify the vision for Delaware is in the works. We continue to pray with business owners all across the state and support them in their community outreaches and political involvements. We have trained intercessors, supported small prayer groups who are praying for America, and prayed with family-focused ministry leaders and their staffs. We have visited Legislative Hall and met with staffers and legislators on many occasions, offering prayer, counsel, and support. We have been releasing prayers over the airways through a Christian radio station reaching all three counties. Our thirty-second prayer spots are releasing blessings and calling the state to prayer.

These are foundations being laid and only some of the highlights. We are learning every city and county has its own issues, strongholds, and territorial spirits. We are in the process of identifying these strongholds, training strategic level intercessors, seeking the strategy and timing of the Lord, and partnering with marketplace and governmental leaders who are ready to occupy the land. This is all part of the strategy for going into a successful prayer initiative over a state.

Hope is growing, and people are responding to the call to prayer. Walls are coming down between churches, and people are beginning to see the path to change. More will be written about this in the future, but I have great excitement about what God is doing in Delaware.

Know the Land and the Enemy

Every "land" is different, and every enemy is unique. Looking again at our Disneyland illustration, we will find two groups of pirates, Captain Hook and the pirates in Never Land and also the Pirates of the Caribbean. They are vastly different.

Fantasyland is home to Never Land where Peter

Pan and the lost boys enjoyed eternal youth. Captain Hook was the overarching, undisputed stronghold of evil controlling Never Land and was Peter Pan's arch enemy. He was neurotic, egotistical, and obsessed with a ticking crocodile. Hook's hatred of Peter drove him to the brink of insanity. In time, Peter Pan took on his adversary and his entire crew and drove them from Never Land forever.

On the other hand, Adventureland is home to the Pirates of the Caribbean where vicious blood thirsty warmongers are glorified in a never-ending saga. The line between good guys and bad guys is blurred, but the point is, just because an enemy bears the same designated title does not mean that its effect on a community is similar or the strategy to remove it will be the same. The land and the enemy are always different, and we need to understand both.

The Lord knows the enemies and the land well. His strategy will be different in every location. To be effective in spiritual warfare, we need to hear His voice and follow His lead. What worked for David when he took out Goliath or for Joshua and his army at the walls of Jericho may not work for our situation.

Detaching from the Stronghold

"Be careful not to make a treaty with those who live in the land where you are going, or they will be a snare among you.

"Break down their altars, smash their sacred stones and cut down their Asherah poles.

"Do not worship any other god, for the LORD, whose name is Jealous, is a jealous God" (Exodus 34:12-14 NIV).

It is possible to pull down the sacred pillars and strongholds of hell controlling our communities. To most effectively stop the backlash before it starts, we must begin by detaching ourselves from their influence. We must stop feeding the boa constrictor and allowing it unhindered multiplication in our lives (see Chapter 5 subtitle, *"When Snakes Enter the Garden"*).

We will probably never pull down a physical altar, but the altars in our minds where our thoughts agree with hell's strongholds in the land must come down. Then we can teach others to do the same.

Let us say the Lord has shown you the pirate controlling your land, or in intercessors vernacular, the overarching demonic stronghold controlling your city is a spirit of death. You can confirm it by looking at the level of violence and murder taking place in your city. In all likelihood, it is rooted in the loss of the value for life as a result of the daily shedding of innocent blood through the abortion industry. However, if you try to go toe-to-toe with the abortion industry, you will face giants in the land you probably are not ready to take on. There are Davids who are called to take down Goliaths, but unless you have an entire army ready to spring into action and chase the enemy out of the country, you will be overrun by the Philistines (see I Samuel Chapter 17).

This is not meant to discredit those gallant warriors who are called to be watchmen on this mountain. We must continue to hold this demonically controlled industry accountable for their actions and pursue every strategy the Lord is giving us to remove this evil from our land. However, to take a stand against the strongman of abortion or the strongman of death as intercessors is not advisable unless the Lord has given you a very clear word, multiple confirmations from those whose authority in the land is greater than yours, a strategy, and an army ready to pursue, drive out, and occupy once Goliath's head has been removed. If all these bases are not covered, then the evil that returns will be much worse than the original enemy you pulled down.

> **"When an unclean spirit goes out of a man, he goes through dry places, seeking rest; and finding none, he says, 'I will return to my house from which I came.'**
> **"And when he comes, he finds it swept and put in order.**
> **"Then he goes and takes with him seven other spirits more wicked than himself, and they enter and dwell there; and the last state of that man is worse than the first" (Luke 11:24-26 NKJV).**

It took ten plagues in Egypt before Pharaoh released the children of Israel from their bondage. We do not know how many plagues it will take or how long the battle will last, but it begins with us and it can begin immediately!

Using the spirit of death as an example, ask:

- Where has the spirit of death had an impact on my life? Have I or has anyone in my family had an abortion or been a part of the abortion industry? Are there acts of violence or murder in my family history? Are their premature deaths in my family?

- Is there hatred in my heart because of these violent actions? Do I hold unforgiveness in my soul as a result? Do I curse those who have caused me harm with my thoughts and words? Do I have a death wish against anyone or for myself?

If these are issues you or your family wrestle with, it is evidence that a stronghold of death not only rules in your city, it has inroads into your life as well. The first order of business is to deal with the enemies on the home front. All of these actions, whether in word, thought, or deed, will be an open door through which the enemy will retaliate. But the greater issue is, if you or your family members are dealing with any of these debilitating problems, you must be set free. They will hold you in a prison of darkness and bitterness until you repent and break off the chains holding you captive. Before you jump into the battle for your city, you must put a stop to the strongholds in your life and family first!

Steps to freedom using the spirit of death as an example:

- **Repent** for yourself and on behalf of others in your family for participating or connecting with death or murder at any level. This includes repenting for anger, unforgiveness, hatred, cursing, and so on.
- **Ask God's forgiveness** for holding onto any offense. Release what was lost. Lay it down at the foot of the cross. Ask the Lord to set you free from the pain and release the loss to Him.
- **Forgive those who have caused you and your family harm.** This can be the most difficult part, especially if there is violence or premature death in your family. You must choose to forgive those responsible, forgive them for hurting you and your family, and bring the offense to the cross and declare it is over. Accept the shed blood of Jesus as payment in full. They owe you nothing.
- **Forgive yourself.** Acknowledge that because of the hurt and pain you have carried, you have hurt others. It is time to lay it down and forgive yourself.
- **Apply Luke 6:28: "Bless those who curse you, pray for those who mistreat you."** If possible, go to the person who hurt you and forgive them. Ask the Lord to soften and heal his or her heart and go in a spirit of humility. Ask God to turn what was intended for evil into much good.
- **Renounce and break** the power of any resulting

curses from your life. Break all agreement with demons associated with this offense and refuse them access into your heart and mind again.

- **Bind it and send it away "No one can enter a strong man's house without first tying him up" (see Mark 3:27 NIV).** Bind the stronghold of death the enemy has placed in your life and send it out the door and away from all that is yours. Give it all to the Lord to become a part of His footstool. Then guard your heart and mind so it does not return.
- **Change your behavior** and occupy with the opposite spirit. Put on love and kindness, walk in grace and forgiveness. Refuse to hate or to come into agreement with evil. Keep your eyes on the Lord and worship Him.
- **When it tries to come back**, recognize it for what it is. Do not go there in your thoughts or words and do not come back into agreement with it. Simply put, do not allow it to breathe the same air you breathe!

No matter what the enemy stronghold is in your city, you will first need to recognize how it is affecting you and others around you. This is the first order of business. When you have broken the grip of hell off your life, it will seem like the darkness has been lifted, the light has come on, and the love of the Lord is free to flow through you again. Once you are free to love and forgive, you can be an extension of God's love to your neighbors and friends. Everyone who learns to love and forgive from your example will be one more roadblock against the inroads from hell coming into your community. By simply loving and forgiving, you can put into motion a chain reaction. People will be drawn to you, and a team of quiet revolution against the powers of hell will begin to form. These first steps will often lead to the next steps. Let the Lord go before you, listen to His voice, and take the ground He is giving you. Little by little you will increase and take possession.

Can it be that easy? First steps are usually the most difficult, but once the ball starts rolling, doors will begin to open and strategies and solutions will begin to come into view.

It is possible to call our nation back to the Lord one state at a time. There will be more steps and greater battles to be fought in Delaware, but the domino effect has already begun. Dream big for your communities, but do not be afraid to start small. With the right strategy, the right team, and an unshakable resolve to stay the course from start to finish, you may discover strategic level intercession is not as scary as it sounds.

Chapter 9
A Strategic Prayer Initiative

The weapons we fight with are not the weapons of the world. On the contrary, they have divine power to demolish strongholds.

(II Corinthians 10:4 NIV)

Heritage International Ministries

When MorningStar Ministries purchased a portion of the former Heritage USA property in 2004, it was in a sad state. The property had been sitting vacant for years after Heritage USA went bankrupt and Hurricane Hugo caused extensive damage in 1989. The restoration process is ongoing and has been immense. But as of this writing, The Grand Hotel has been restored and is being used as a hotel and conference center, and the courtyard interior hotel rooms are being converted into condominiums. The atrium, formerly the hotel lobby, is now MorningStar Fellowship Church. Main Street is home to the Book Store, Café, MorningStar University, and various ministries and shops. The Tower is still waiting to be reclaimed and made into a "refirement" center for the 55+ generation. The entire building complex has been renamed Heritage International Ministries (H.I.M.).

The buildings could be restored, painted, and cleaned up on the outside, but the land and structures needed to be spiritually restored too. There were frequent reports to the intercession department from people sensing curses, witchcraft, and occultism surrounding the property. We bumped up against the strongholds hindering the ministry in various ways and felt that a spiritual cleansing was needed.

The Plan

Rick Joyner calls July our sabbatical month when all church activities are suspended, including Sunday services. Since the church was empty and there were no conferences or meetings taking place, July was a perfect time for a strategic prayer focus. One summer a few years ago, the intercession department leader and I constructed a multi-layered plan to address five demonic strongholds still dominating the property. The department leader had already brought some insight to the church body about how MorningStar was being impacted because of these strongholds. By working together, we were able to construct a plan that would be both effective and safe. During the month of July, we focused our attention on redeeming the property through a strategic prayer initiative. We were given the use of an apartment in the H.I.M. conference center where I stayed during the month of July to fast, pray, and oversee the prayer teams. Our plan did not include reclaiming the Tower. It would require a different plan and strategy and was not part of the Lord's agenda at that time.

I wrote a *Redeeming the Land* prayer, and it was presented with our strategic plan for the month of July to Rick. He gave us his blessing to proceed and do all the Lord was leading us to do. The following is a brief overview of the strategy and how we walked it out.

The Strategy

Blessing the Land: We began in June with a small team that prayer-walked the property releasing blessings, similar to our strategy in Washington, D.C. It was a powerful and anointed time taking place early each morning and lasting about an hour. Before each walk, we took turns leading a prayer that included putting on the armor of the Lord from Ephesians chapter 6 and extending a prayer covering over our families and loved ones. John Kilpatrick wrote a wonderful prayer called "Speaking a Blessing" that we used frequently at the start of each prayer-walk. We ended our walk with another prayer to safeguard ourselves and loved ones from any demonic backlash.

The Teams: We divided the intercessors into teams.

We decided to continue our early morning prayer-walk through July but would shift from merely blessing the land to occupying and enforcing prayer declarations. Another team was assigned to prayer-walk inside the buildings, blessing and occupying with prophetic prayers, Scriptures, and worship. A small team of intercession leaders met weekly to pray land-cleansing prayers to break off the sins of the land. A prayer shield team was appointed to pray for all the other team members. This was our most important team.

Warfare Team Briefing: On July 1, we brought the warfare teams together for training and a briefing of our strategy. We gave an overview of the five strongholds and how they gain access into our personal lives. Our strategy was to detach ourselves from these spirits and give them no foothold in our lives. The biggest stronghold we had to contend with was Leviathan.

Job 41 describes this enemy well. Leviathan is a powerful destroyer of property, lives, and health. Leviathan's stronghold is pride (see Job 41:34). In Job chapter 42, Leviathan was defeated when Job humbled himself and repented for speaking about things he knew nothing about (see Job 42:3-6). According to Job chapter 41, Leviathan is king over all who are proud. Humility and obedience were the weapons that would defeat pride.

According to Isaiah 27:1, Leviathan is called the

"wriggling serpent" that will be killed at the end of time. Leviathan's rule on the earth will not be stopped until the end of time. However, we had the authority to dismantle its stronghold over the H.I.M. property. In the same way that my family sent fear away from our home (see Chapter 5 subtitle, "How to Rule and Reign in Your Garden"), we could dismantle a stronghold where we had been given authority to do so. We can:

- **Repent:** Ask the Lord's forgiveness for allowing the unholy sprit a place in our lives and church.
- **Stop serving it:** Stop feeding it, honoring it, bowing to its authority, and coming under its rule.
- **Bind it and send it away:** Send it out the door and away from everything we have authority over.
- **Close the door behind it so it will not come back:** Once we understand what open door is allowing rulers and principalities to gain access and dominion, close it and set guards at the door so it cannot come back.
- **Change our behavior and occupy with opposite spirit:** Invite peace to rule instead of demons, and the fruit of the Spirit to be in operation.

- **When demonic rulers try to come back:** Do not allow them to breathe the same air we breathe!

I wrote a *Prayer of Repentance* aimed at severing all attachment to the five strongholds we were dealing with. For the purpose of this writing, I have only listed two that we broke agreement with that day. This book is not intended to be used to identify demonic strongholds. There are far more knowledgeable people and ministries that can describe and identify them better than I whose books I use frequently. In addition, I prefer not to give the enemy too much attention or credit, instead giving the Lord the glory for His awesome deliverance.

Prayer of Repentance

Lord, as we prepare ourselves to engage in this awesome battle, we confess we have been as much a part of the problem as those we are praying for. You give us authority against the demonic realm because of Your great love for Your children and Your hatred for the enemy. Thank You for the shed blood of Jesus that gives us access to Your throne and authority against the powers of hell.

Where we have agreed with Leviathan, we repent for giving place to pride, superiority, haughtiness, boasting arrogance, discord, division, ungodly communication, twisting words, slander, gossip, accusation, and lies. Forgive us for our self-serving agendas and attitudes, and our desire to manipulate and control others into serving ourselves instead of You. Forgive us for thinking more highly of ourselves than we ought and for not considering others as more important than ourselves. We repent and lay down our need for reputation, wanting to be served, being competitive and jealous when others achieve and excel, and forgive us for dishonoring and rebelling against authority.

Where we have agreed with witchcraft, we repent for rebellion against authority and each other, for manipulating and controlling others through intimidation, ridicule, guilt, blame, shame, flattery, or seduction, for causing our brothers and sisters to compromise their faith morally or spiritually, for challenging leadership, and for opposing true purity and holiness.

We exchange these evil attributes by putting on humility, unity with one another, love, and forgiveness. We choose a life devoted to Christ and to each other, to be kind, teachable, patient, honoring, and serving with integrity. We lay down our lives for each other, preferring the other above ourselves. We seek true wisdom from above, righteousness, grace, peace, truth, and faith. We put on true spiritual authority, and we trust the Lord to accomplish His will and purposes on earth.

We choose this day to put our hands to the plow and not look back. We take up the mantle and with it the calling to press on until the battle is won or until the Lord releases us. We will not give up, turn back, give in, bow down, or come under the enemy's rule. Our lives are not our own, we have been bought with a price and redeemed by the blood of Jesus to bring about His kingdom rule on earth. We submit ourselves again to You, Lord Jesus, and thank You for the privilege of partnering with You in this awesome adventure as we begin to advance the Lordship of Jesus Christ at Heritage International Ministries.

July 2 notes from my journal: *In a vision a few weeks ago, I saw the torso of some type of demonic creature. Attached to its chest were several tubes that reminded me of umbilical cords. They started at the top of its ribcage and extended all the way down its belly. These were feeding tubes, and something was flowing through them into the creature's chest and belly. I felt that people who were coming into agreement and serving these strongholds on the land were feeding this creature and giving it authority to stay.*

Then I saw someone take large clamps to clamp off the tubes, blocking the flow of agreement with the enemy. I knew the Lord was showing me that when people stop serving these demonic strongholds, it would cut off the supply lines and die. Our prayers of consecration and declaration were like clamps over the enemy's feeding tubes.

Prayer Shield team briefing: I explained to this team that their most important assignment was to pray for the warfare team, to lock shields around them. Our focus was not only the warfare team but their families and all that was important to them. I used the Scripture from I Samuel 14:7 that describes Jonathan's armor-bearer as an example for their role.

> **"Do all that you have in mind," his armor-bearer said. "Go ahead; I am with you heart and soul."**
> **The men of the outpost shouted to Jonathan and his armor-bearer, "Come up to us and we'll teach you a lesson." So Jonathan said to his armor-bearer, "Climb up after me; the LORD has given them into the hand of Israel.**
> **Jonathan climbed up, using his hands and feet, with his armor-bearer right behind him. The Philistines fell before Jonathan, and his armor-bearer followed and killed behind him.**
> **In that first attack Jonathan and his armor-bearer killed some twenty men in an area of about half an acre (I Samuel 14:7; 12-14 NIV)."**

I reminded them that consecration through prayer, repentance, and cleansing from any inroads coming from the spirits we were dealing with would help protect them from demonic backlash. This team would be standing in the gap for someone else, and as a result, they could become a target of the enemy. To keep themselves and their families safe, the full armor of God as described in Ephesians chapter 6 needed to be securely in place. I felt it was necessary to set the bar high, so I advised them they needed to apply the following guidelines with that in mind:

- A prayer covering: Enlist prayer partners who would pray for them regularly
- Their spouse's blessings for this assignment
- A lifestyle of worship, prayer, and regular Bible reading
- Honor the Lord in their homes
- Honor the Lord with their lifestyles
- Deal with any area of sin in their lives

Without their prayer covering, the warfare team would be vulnerable to a counter attack coming from these strongholds towards them and their families. Jonathan would not have been able to go in and attack the Philistines without his armour-bearer. His accomplishments were far greater because his armour-bearer fought alongside of him.

July 6 notes from my journal: *Prior to the kick-off I had a vision of heavy rain pouring down over MorningStar. The rain was coming in waves. Then I saw an army of warriors advance on horseback clothed in full armor. I could see everything very clearly: their breastplates, helmets, swords, shields. They were strong and powerful. One of the soldiers ran up and held his shield over me to protect me from the rain that was like a slow moving wall of water. After the rain passed it was dry, the sun was shining down brightly* *and everything appeared to be clean and white. Even the horses were white, where before everything looked grey.*

The kick-off prayer: Some of the wording in the prayers I write will occasionally reflect a book I am reading at the time. I was reading Cindy Trimm's The Rules of Engagement so some of the language in the following prayer is reminiscent of the Prayer of Activation from her book.

Redeeming the Land

As Ambassadors of the Lord Jesus Christ and as His official representatives here on earth, we announce to the visible and invisible realms that Heritage International Ministries (H.I.M.) is coming under the authority of kingdom of heaven now, and God's plans and purposes for these sacred grounds is preeminent, the only authority we recognize.

We submit H.I.M. to the Lordship of Jesus Christ and declare we are subject to the authority and rule of Christ alone. H.I.M. exists to glorify God here on earth and to expand the kingdom of heaven in this nation and throughout the earth. This ministry is an extension of the kingdom purposes of God, and it is under the covering and protection of the King of kings and Lord of lords. We stand on the Word of the Living God that says no weapon formed against us shall prosper! We repent and break agreement with fear, doubt, unbelief, and failure. We stand on the Word of God that says the same Spirit that raised Christ from the dead dwells in us! We put on kingdom authority, clothe ourselves with the full armor of God, take up the weapons of warfare, and take back what is rightfully ours.

We build a hedge of protection that cannot be breached and draw a bloodline that cannot be crossed around H.I.M. and all related ministries on this property. As this line is drawn, we deny the enemy access to these buildings and all who gather here. We command that demonic interruptions in the affairs of this ministry end now. The blood of Jesus covers us, and we are hidden from the enemy's tactics. We rest in the safety and protection of the Lord Jesus Christ.

We are free from every curse, debt, sickness, and bondage that has come upon H.I.M. through the kingdom of darkness. We declare all who are associated with this ministry are free from demonic influence. We cancel all witchcraft prayers, spells, curses, including critical, unjust words spoken against H.I.M. pastors, officers, staff, teachers, employees, volunteers, members, associates, and friends. We reverse the curse resulting from these utterances and decree that they will not stand, they will not take root, and they will not come to pass.

We declare that we live our lives by faith in the Son of God. We refuse to bow down to the enemy's tactics or give them a place in our hearts. Though we walk through the water or the flame, You, Lord, are with us, and we will not be moved! We walk as children of the Most High and ambassadors of His kingdom. All things must line up according to the favor of the Lord that rests on H.I.M. and according to our calling and purpose in this hour. We walk from glory to glory in the victory that is ours, and we enforce God's full purposes for H.I.M. in this hour. In the mighty name of Jesus our Lord and Savior, AMEN!

The Kick Off

After everyone was trained, briefed, prayed up, sanctified, and delivered, we were ready to proceed. On the afternoon of July 6, the teams gathered together with their banners, flags, shofars, and musical instruments. It had been raining hard most of the day, but we prayed for the clouds to part and the sun to shine. The rain stopped just as the team was arriving. Our worship leaders led the procession with their musical instruments and songs of praise. I began by reading our *Redeeming the Land* prayer, and everyone responded with shouts of agreement and songs and praise. There were no restrictions on how we did this. Everyone was allowed to dance, wave their flags, blow their shofars, and enjoy a time of unhindered worship.

The property boundaries were identified, and we did something similar to a Jericho march around the entire perimeter. We had already been walking around the property lines blessing the land during the month of June, so this walk was for pulling down the demonic walls and gates and announcing to the seen and unseen realms that the kingdom of heaven was taking over at H.I.M. We stopped on the north, south, east, and west points of the property to read our Redeeming the Land prayer, sing praises, read Scriptures, and make declarations. We were a loud, happy, and exuberant group!

July 7 notes from my journal: *In a vision this afternoon, I saw the spiritual battleground we prayed over last night during our kick-off prayer procession. I could see smoke rising from the property as if it had been bombed. I saw craters where our prayers and declarations were like guided missiles that had devastated the enemy's camp. The vision kept switching to different locations wherever bombs hit the ground, causing massive craters where huge insects had been hiding. Their nests had been blown up, and only a few stragglers remained. As the vision was focusing in on the craters, I saw an enormous eye from something that looked reptilian. It appeared we had destroyed most of leviathan's servants on the land on the first phase of our battle plan.*

2nd vision: I saw a huge wasp, 15 feet long or more, lying dead on its back. Several people stood around it and they were moving its legs and its wings as though they were checking to see if it was really dead. I had the feeling they didn't believe that it was dead, but were in fact coaxing it to get back up again. I prayed we would be like David when he killed Goliath with nothing but a sling and a stone, and follow through by chopping off his head. I prayed, "Lord, let us not resurrect this thing with unbelief or by going back to our old ways!"

On the days following our kick-off prayer, the teams met at different times to focus attention on their assignments. The early morning prayer-walk continued much the same as it had started in June. The team assigned to prayer-walk the inside of the facility met several times a week to pray over and bless the offices, hotel rooms, shops, schools, and other ministries, including the Atrium where MorningStar church took place. The land cleansing team met twice a week in the evenings in the warfare room to repent for the sins that had taken place on the land. The prayer shield team met weekly to pray together for all of the teams. They were also responsible to pray for them daily during their own prayer time. In the evenings, I invited anyone who could to join me for fellowship and prayer in the apartment.

All of the teams stayed faithful to their assignments for the entire month. At the beginning of the month, I prayed it would not rain again until we completed our assignment on the last day of July. I ended my fast on the last day of the month. We got together on Main Street for a praise celebration and communion, and then we went to the apartment for a potluck. As we were finishing up our meal and sharing praise reports and answers to prayer, lightning and thunder cracked through the sky, and a heavy downpour swept over the property. It was not until then that I realized it had not rained since our kick-off. Not only had the Lord answered our prayer to hold back the rain during our prayer initiative, but I felt it was a confirmation that the land had been cleansed.

Looking back, I believe the focused prayer during the month of July helped advance the process of healing and restoration at H.I.M. It was only the first in a series of intensive prayer assignments that continue to this day. The Lord protected the teams and their families. There were no unusual sicknesses, injuries, or fatalities before, during, or after the assignment.

We have seen a major shift in the leadership and staff at MorningStar, which often happens following strategic level intercession. As the dust settles, I believe we are seeing a new day dawning. Rick Joyner is having some of the most profound prophetic experiences he has ever had, and a higher level of the prophetic gift is being released to the church body. Were strongholds pulled down by this strategy? There are strong opinions on both sides of the fence. I am sure far more than meets the eye was accomplished, and if we keep ourselves free from the influence of these strongholds, H.I.M. will continue to take great strides forward toward her destiny.

CHAPTER 10
Final Thoughts

There is a time for everything, and a season for every activity under the heavens.

(Ecclesiastes 3:1 NIV)

Stay Balanced

The changing tide in intercession has been marked with extremes. I am still in the process of learning how to keep a balanced prayer life. During my journey, I have noticed that some of my most effective prayers were birthed in my greatest trials.

In I Samuel chapter 1, we read the account of Hannah, who was desperate for a son. In bitterness of soul, she wept and prayed and promised that if the Lord would give her a son, she would give him back to the Lord all the days of his life. She had been pressed to the point of desperation and then gave back to the Lord what she desired most. When we finally get to the point where we realize "it's not about me" but rather it is all about the Lord and His kingdom, true intercession will result. Self-centered prayers produce self-centered people. A God-centered prayer life will produce heartfelt prayers that will get the Lord's attention. It is the only way to avoid falling into the religious ditch running on either side of the balanced path that intercessors must walk. In this chapter, I will tell you about some of the extremes I have encountered while learning these lessons.

Avoid the Pitfalls of Extremes

Not every call to prayer is a call to war. At the heart of true intercession is communion with the Father. Intercession occurs when we release in prayer what we have heard while in His presence. If we do not take time to be in His presence, we will not know what we are supposed to release through intercession. **"Very early in the morning, while it was still dark, Jesus got up, left the house and went off to a solitary place, where he prayed" (Mark 1:35 NIV).** Should we do any less?

Worship the Lord and meditate on His Word. This is where we become one with Him and His purposes on the earth. In this place He shares His secrets with His beloved. Cultivating a lifestyle of worship will keep us balanced, on target, and able to pray powerful, anointed prayers. Whether praying for a harvest to be plentiful, a nation to return to God, or a stronghold to come down, it must begin and end with the Creator of all things. He alone has the solution to every need and the strategy to unravel the plans of the enemy.

Those who war after principalities, powers, and rulers without seeking the Lord first will find themselves fighting a never-ending battle. For them, every prayer session becomes a calling card to wage war against the demonic realm. Once they enter a battle from this position, the enemy will keep them at war and critical of everyone who is not warring with them. They often become disenchanted with the church and frustrated with the body of Christ instead of growing more in love with the Lord and His flock. Their worldview becomes distorted, and rather than gaining great victories, they sadly become the objects of great deception.

Does this mean we should never direct our prayers against the demonic realm? No, but we need to avoid the pitfalls of extremes. Our focus should always be the Lord. Seek Him first, and He will lead us into battle with a strategy for victory.

On the other hand, once we have found this glorious place of worship, keep in mind there is a time and season for everything, including mountaintop experiences. The mountaintop is the most wonderful place we can be, but guard against getting stuck here too. Deception can occur on both sides of the fence. Take what you see on the mountaintop and birth it through mountain-moving intercession.

Be careful not to allow the fear of man to keep you "hidden" in worship. There is a higher call. It is found in I John 4:7-8, **"Dear friends, let us love one another, for love comes from God. Everyone who loves has been born of God and knows God. Whoever does not love does not know God, because God is love" (NIV).** If we are going to love people, introduce them to the Lord, and set them free from sin, then we have to come down from the mountaintop to be with them.

There is No Silver Bullet

Wouldn't you love to find someone who could teach you how to pray powerful, anointed prayers that would guarantee victory every time you prayed? While there are certain disciplines and prayers to make us better intercessors, we must also recognize there is no silver bullet. What I mean is, there is no specific type of prayer, special Scripture, or anointed person that will cause breakthrough every time. Mighty weapons are being released to the body of Christ today that can pull down strongholds (see II Corinthians 10:4). As with all weapons, they are most effective when deployed in the proper way and the right time under the direction of the One who is in command of the battle. When the Lord is directing our battles, His weapon of choice will be accompanied with great authority to pull down strongholds and break the chains of injustice from people and nations.

Legislating from the courts of heaven, blessing and redeeming the land, apostolic decrees and declarations are just a few of the mighty weapons released to the body of Christ in these last days. These high-level spiritual warfare prayers are powerful weapons, reminding me of the war strategy our military used years ago called "Shock and Awe." We should learn how to deploy all the weapons the Lord gives us, but we also need to guard against building a doctrine around them. They are just some of the artillery in the Master's wide-ranging arsenal. He alone knows which one is needed and when to use it.

According to Ephesians 6:18, we should be well-versed in all kinds of prayers, **"And pray in the Spirit on all occasions with all kinds of prayers and requests. With this in mind, be alert and always keep on praying for all of the Lord's people" (NIV).** Let us look at this Scripture phrase by phrase:

1. **Pray in the Spirit** – Disengage from carnal thinking and allow the Spirit of the Lord opportunity to guide and direct your prayers. All aspects of an intercessor's prayer life must flow from the Throne Room, not just when praying in tongues. While worshiping, meditating, declaring, legislating, blessing, or warring, we must be both kings and priests through the realm of the Spirit.

2. **On all occasions** – There is no wrong time for prayer. An intercessor needs to be ready in season and out to pray on all occasions—in good times and bad, in war and in peace, for friends and foes. The Lord not only heals people, He will heal guinea pigs and salamanders just to demonstrate

His love for the world. He will stop hurricanes, level mountains, and cause it to rain if someone will intercede. There is no awkward time or place for prayer. The Lord is ready and willing at all times.

3. **Pray all kinds of prayers** – Learn all the disciplines of prayer, starting with the prayers recorded in The Bible. Study the great prayer warriors and their prayers throughout the ages. Learn all you can about their prayer lives and how God answered and moved in their generations. Discover all the tools of prayer God is releasing today. Be ready at all times to pray the right prayer from the Father's heart into each situation.

4. **Be alert** – While most of the world sleeps, witches and warlocks are conjuring up spells and releasing curses during the night watch. Stay alert at all times, even while sleeping by allowing the Lord to speak to you in dreams or by getting up in the early hours of the morning to intercede when the Lord calls.

5. **Keep on praying** – It is exciting to pray when the answers are swift, and we can see immediate results. But when the promise takes years to fulfill, it is easier give up or get discouraged. When we have done everything, prayed every kind of prayer, confessed with our mouth what we do not yet see, and still nothing happens, there is only one thing to do. KEEP ON PRAYING.

6. **For all of the Lord's people** – Break out of the mold, stretch your faith, and pray for more people. The guy in the car next to you on the freeway probably needs prayer. Storm the gates of heaven on his behalf even though he may never know why his day is suddenly blessed. He may be one step closer to receiving Jesus as the Lord of his life because of your prayer.

I have been in meetings where fervent prayer warriors shout, dance, and shatter strongholds with powerful declarations. I have also been in prayer meetings where simple believers pray from a book of prayers. The Lord can move mightily in both settings, because He looks at the heart and responds to faith more than words and actions. We must learn to connect to the Lord in all kinds of environments and with all kinds of prayers. However, there is something much more important than being well-versed in all kinds of prayers; we must know the One who taught us to pray.

Jesus wants a bride who will spend time with Him and seek to know His heart and His will. We can excel in intercessory strategy, know all the right words, and lead a disciplined prayer life, yet still not know Him. Matthew 7:22-23 is a sober warning, **"Many will say to Me in that day, 'Lord, Lord, have we not prophesied in Your name, cast out demons in Your name, and done many wonders in Your name?' And then I will declare to them, 'I never knew you; depart from Me, you who practice lawlessness!'" (NKJV)**

Is There a Safe Place?

Warfare is fought with many weapons and on many fronts. Praise, worship, blessing, decrees, Scripture reading, etc., are all powerful weapons the Lord has given us. They will challenge demons and rattle the gates of hell as surely as any other weapon of war. Thinking you are under the enemy's radar by blessing the land and praising the Lord is not a safe assumption, unless it is the Lord's plan. Remember that our weapons are not carnal, but mighty through God. Carnal weapons are weapons contrived by man. Mighty weapons are Divine weapons given to us by the Lord and are the only weapons able to pull down a stronghold. If the Lord sends us into battle singing praises, walls will come down. If He sends us to war enforcing the laws of the kingdom of heaven over the lies of the devil, the demonic realm will flee. But if the Lord is not sending us, it will not matter what kind of prayer we use. Our prayers will be empty and powerless, and may do more to alert the enemy to our position than achieve a great victory.

The only safe place is to be **"in the Beloved" (see Ephesians 1:6 NKJV)**, listening to His voice and doing what He is commanding us to do. He will not send a novice into battle. He always takes us by the safest route first, and then proceeds to train and align us with His generals and His army. Remember the lessons from Exodus 23—little by little we take and occupy the land as the Lord goes before us.

Titles and Positions

The five-fold ministry recorded in Ephesians 4:11 is being restored as apostles come into prominence and join the ranks of the prophets, evangelists, pastors, and teachers. There is much debate surrounding the Scriptural role of the apostle. I will not attempt to join that discussion other than to say that titles do matter. They are like badges of authority in the spirit realm. Authority in prayer is increased when accompanied with apostolic order. Apostolic prayers are not more authoritative because they are more declarative in nature, but because the Lord sees and honors the gifts He gives. Demons recognize this too.

I attended an ordination service several months ago and experienced a beautiful vision during worship just before the ordination took place. I saw the Lord laying His hand on the shoulders of the people who were going to be ordained. His head was bowed, and He whispered prayers in their ears. Then I saw angels coming behind Him with gifts wrapped in plain brown paper tied with cord. They handed these gifts to all the people who were being prayed for. After this vision, the ordination proceeded in exactly the same manner I had just seen in the spirit realm. After the pastor laid hands on their shoulders and prayed for each person, prophets came forward and prophesied over each one. Their prophetic words were like gifts that would set them in their new places of authority. I understood from this vision just how important this ordination service was to the Lord. He was moving powerfully, imparting a new level of ministry and authority over each person. There is an authority structure and order in the church and great authority accompanies those who receive these designated mantles of office.

It is also important to remember that with great authority comes greater responsibility. Even our idle words carry authority. James warns, **"Not many of you should become teachers, my fellow believers, because you know that we who teach will be judged more strictly" (James 3:1 NIV).** The verses that follow warn about keeping the tongue in check. Verse 10 expresses a strong warning, **"Out of the same mouth come praise and cursing. My brothers and sisters, this should not be."** This chapter in James was written to the teacher, the last office mentioned in the five-fold ministry, but it should be the standard for all of the ministry offices spoken of in Ephesians 4:11.

There is an Army Arising

This next generation of youth is called to be the dread champions. Those of us who have been in the battle for decades can either step aside or pave the way. They need seasoned leaders to follow into battle, but they must not be held back. The Lord showed me we are like parents riding bikes with babies sitting in infant seats behind us. I saw a baby climbing out of the infant seat and reaching for the handlebars. They will be content to be in infant seats for a short time, but they need to be allowed to grow up and learn to drive. The young are ready to rumble. We must not keep them from their destinies or hold them back, or they will step over us and jump in the driver's seat without the knowledge and experience we have to give them. They are fearless and ready to take over. Instead of teaching them what they can't do, teach them what they can do. Give them all of the weapons of warfare and show them how to take back what the enemy has stolen from their generation. We must guide them like gifted children who will one day surpass us. They will make mistakes along the way just as we did, but we must give them the latitude to learn.

Scriptures to Hang on Your Refrigerator Door

Do not jump on every "wind of doctrine" that comes your way claiming a new, sure-fire method to crack open the heavens or take out the enemy. Know the Scriptures and exercise discernment. Every time a new kind of intercessory prayer comes along, I turn to my favorite verses to help keep me in balance. They not only remind me who I am, but Whose I am.

> **"If I speak in the tongues of men or of angels, but do not have love, I am only a resounding gong or a clanging cymbal.**
>
> **If I have the gift of prophecy and can fathom all mysteries and all knowledge, and if I have a faith that can move mountains, but do not have love, I am nothing.**
>
> **If I give all I possess to the poor and give over my body to hardship that I may boast, but do not have love, I gain nothing.**

Love is patient, love is kind. It does not envy, it does not boast, it is not proud.
It does not dishonor others, it is not self-seeking, it is not easily angered, it keeps no record of wrongs.
Love does not delight in evil but rejoices with the truth. It always protects, always trusts, always hopes, always perseveres.
Love never fails. But where there are prophecies, they will cease; where there are tongues, they will be stilled; where there is knowledge, it will pass away.
For we know in part and we prophesy in part, but when completeness comes, what is in part disappears.
When I was a child, I talked like a child, I thought like a child, I reasoned like a child. When I became a man, I put the ways of childhood behind me.
For now we see only a reflection as in a mirror; then we shall see face to face. Now I know in part; then I shall know fully, even as I am fully known.
And now these three remain: faith, hope and love. But the greatest of these is love" (I Corinthians 13 NIV).

"Let not the wise man glory in his wisdom, let not the mighty man glory in his might, nor let the rich man glory in his riches;

But let him who glories, glory in this, that he understands and knows Me, that I am the Lord, exercising lovingkindness, judgement, and righteousness in the earth. For in these I delight" says the Lord (Jeremiah 9-23-24 NKJV).

"Here is the conclusion of the matter: fear God and keep his commandments, for this is the duty of all mankind" (see Ecclesiastes 12:13 NIV).

"He has shown you, O mortal, what is good. And what does the LORD require of you? To act justly and to love mercy and to walk humbly with your God" (Micah 6:8 NIV).

"Blessed is the one who does not walk in step with the wicked or stand in the way that sinners take or sit in the company of mockers,

but whose delight is in the law of the LORD, and who meditates on his law day and night.

That person is like a tree planted by streams of water, which yields its fruit in season and whose leaf does not wither—whatever they do prospers" (Psalm 1:1-3 NIV).

Jesus replied: "Love the Lord your God with all your heart and with all your soul

and with all your mind."

This is the first and greatest commandment. And the second is like it: "Love your neighbor as yourself."

All the Law and the Prophets hang on these two commandments" (Matthew 22:37-40 NIV).

"You do not have because you do not ask God.

When you ask, you do not receive, because you ask with wrong motives, that you may spend it on what you get on your pleasures" (James 4:2-3 NIV).

"The prayer of a righteous person is powerful and effective.

Elijah was a human being, even as we are. He prayed earnestly that it would not rain, and it did not rain on the land for three and a half years.

Again he prayed, and the heavens gave rain, and the earth produced its crops" (see James 5:16-18 NIV).

Get Invested!

Get invested with the people and the places God is sending you to. Develop covenant relationships and learn to lay down your life for your friends. Be a part of their lives, their business, and their communities.

Engage with the Lord in their surroundings. Hear His heart for them, and wait for Him to reveal who their enemies are, and He will give you the strategy to set them free. When you have compassion for the people God sends to you, you will have an inroad into their world to pray powerful anointed prayers on their behalf.

When David and his men returned to Ziklag and saw all that belonged to them had been burned or taken captive, they wept until they had no more strength to weep. Then David strengthened himself in the Lord, inquired of Him, and set out in pursuit to overtake and recover all that had been stolen (see I Samuel 30). Your family and neighbors are being assaulted on every front. The flood of darkness and evil coming into the nations is increasing. We are at a crossroad where right and wrong have been skewed, and religious freedom and biblical values are hanging in the balance. God is looking for someone to recognize who the real enemy is and stand in the gap.

The call to pray earth-shattering prayers that will change the course of history is not directed to just a few dedicated intercessors. The prayers of all the righteous are powerful and effective (see James 5:16). The invitation is extended to all who are called to take part in the Marriage Supper of the Lamb.

Take A Stand!

It is time to take a stand! This is where the rubber meets the road, where you draw a line in the sand and say to the evil in your world, "ENOUGH!" Fire the devil, and tell him he is no longer in charge of your affairs. You are through listening to his lies and obeying his demands. He is no longer a fixture in your house, and you are no longer his servant. Throw off the shackles, rise above the muck, and get your wet suit on and jump in. Pursue, overtake, and recover all for the King and His kingdom! Age is not a factor, gender does not matter, titles do not qualify you, and carefully crafted prayers are not what the Lord is looking for. Love the Lord with all your heart and your neighbor as yourself (see Luke 10:27). Then follow Him into battle, occupy what He gives you, and you will be well on your way to becoming one of the dread champions, a world-class intercessor in the making.

"For if you remain silent at this time, relief and deliverance for the Jews (all of the Lord's people!) **will arise from another place, but you and your father's family will perish. And who knows but that you have come to your royal position for such a time as this?" (Esther 4:14 NIV)**

APPENDIX

Scripture References

Scripture References – unless otherwise noted, references are from the New International Version of the Bible.

ESV – English Standard Version

KJV – King James Version

NIV – New International Version

NKJV – New King James Version

Introduction

Galatians 2:20: "I have been crucified with Christ and I no longer live, but Christ lives in me. The life I now live in the body, I live by faith in the Son of God, who loved me and gave himself for me."

Chapter One

Jeremiah 29:11: "For I know the plans I have for you," declares the Lord, "plans to prosper you and not to harm you, plans to give you hope and a future."

II Chronicles 7:14: "If my people, who are called by my name, will humble themselves and pray and seek my face and turn from their wicked ways, then I will hear from heaven, and I will forgive their sin and will heal their land."

I Peter 5:8: "Be alert and of sober mind. Your enemy the devil prowls around like a roaring lion looking for someone to devour."

Proverbs 29:18, KJV: "Where there is no vision, the people perish"

Romans 4:17: "I have made you a father of many nations." He is our father in the sight of God, in whom he believed—the God who gives life to the dead and calls into being things that were not."

Revelation 3:11: "I am coming soon. Hold on to what you have, so that no one will take your crown."

Chapter Two

Isaiah 41:13: "For I am the Lord, your God, who takes hold of your right hand and says to you, 'Do not fear, I will help you.'"

Luke 11:2-4, KJV: "Our Father which art in

heaven, Hallowed be thy name. Thy kingdom come. Thy will be done, as in heaven, so in earth. Give us day by day our daily bread. And forgive us our sins; for we also forgive every one that is indebted to us. And lead us not into temptation; but deliver us from evil."

II Corinthians 11:14: "And no wonder, for Satan himself masquerades as an angel of light."

Leviticus 19:31, ESV: "Do not turn to mediums or necromancers; do not seek them out, and so make yourselves unclean by them: I am the Lord your God."

Deuteronomy 18:10-12, ESV: "There shall not be found among you anyone who burns his son or his daughter as an offering, anyone who practices divination or tells fortunes or interprets omens, or a sorcerer or a charmer or a medium or a necromancer or one who inquires of the dead, for whoever does these things is an abomination to the Lord. And because of these abominations the Lord your God is driving them out before you."

I John 4:1, ESV: "Beloved, do not believe every spirit, but test the spirits to see whether they are from God, for many false prophets have gone out into the world."

I Timothy 4:1, ESV: "Now the Spirit expressly says that in later times some will depart from the faith by devoting themselves to deceitful spirits and teachings of demons."

I Chronicles 10:13, ESV: "So Saul died for his breach of faith. He broke faith with the Lord in that he did not keep the command of the Lord, and also consulted a medium, seeking guidance."

James 3:16: "For where you have envy and selfish ambition, there you find disorder and every evil practice."

I Corinthians 12:8-11, NKJV: "For to one is given the word of wisdom through the Spirit, to another the word of knowledge through the same Spirit, to another faith by the same Spirit, to another gifts of healings by the same Spirit, to another the working of miracles, to another prophecy, to another discerning of spirits, to another different kinds of tongues, to another the interpretation of tongues. But one and the same Spirit works all these things, distributing to each one individually as He wills."

I Corinthians 14:26, NKJV: "How is it then, brethren? Whenever you come together, each of you has a psalm, has a teaching, has a tongue, has a revelation, has an interpretation. Let all things be done for edification."

Chapter Three

Psalm 119:147: "I rise before dawn and cry for help; I have put my hope in your word."

Luke 10:19: "I have given you authority

to trample on snakes and scorpions and to overcome all the power of the enemy; nothing will harm you."

Ephesians 2:2, KJV: "Wherein in time past ye walked according to the course of this world, according to the prince of the power of the air, the spirit that now worketh in the children of disobedience."

Ephesians 6:12: "For our struggle is not against flesh and blood, but against the rulers, against the authorities, against the powers of this dark world and against the spiritual forces of evil in the heavenly realms."

Joshua 3:5, NKJV: "And Joshua said to the people, 'Sanctify yourselves, for tomorrow the LORD will do wonders among you.'"

Joshua 5:15: "The commander of the LORD's army replied, 'Take off your sandals, for the place where you are standing is holy.' And Joshua did so."

Joshua 6:3-5: "March around the city once with all the armed men. Do this for six days. Have seven priests carry trumpets of rams' horns in front of the ark. On the seventh day, march around the city seven times, with the priests blowing the trumpets. When you hear them sound a long blast on the trumpets, have the whole army give a loud shout; then the wall of the city will collapse and the army will go up, everyone straight in."

II Samuel 5:12: "And David realized that the LORD had established him as king over Israel, and that He had exalted his kingdom for the sake of His people Israel."

Chapter Four

Proverbs 4:18: "The path of the righteous is like the first gleam of dawn, shining ever brighter till the full light of day."

II Chronicles 7:14: "If my people, who are called by my name, will humble themselves and pray and seek my face and turn from their wicked ways, then I will hear from heaven, and I will forgive their sin and will heal their land."

Joshua 6:10: "But Joshua had commanded the army, 'Do not give a war cry, do not raise your voices, do not say a word until the day I tell you to shout. Then shout!'"

I Samuel 17:45-47: "You come against me with sword and spear and javelin, but I come against you in the name of the Lord Almighty, the God of the armies of Israel, whom you have defied. This day the LORD will deliver you into my hands, and I'll strike you down and cut off your head. This very day I will give the carcasses of the Philistine army to the birds and the wild animals, and the whole world will know that there is a God in Israel. All those gathered here will know that it is not by sword or spear that the LORD saves; for the battle is the LORD's, and he will give all of you into our hands"

Romans 15:4: "For everything that was written in the past was written to teach us, so that through the endurance taught in the Scriptures and the encouragement they provide we might have hope."

I Corinthians 10:11: "These things happened to them as examples and were written down as warnings for us, on whom the culmination of the ages has come."

Exodus 23:20-33: "See, I am sending an angel ahead of you to guard you along the way and to bring you to the place I have prepared.

"Pay attention to him and listen to what he says. Do not rebel against him; he will not forgive your rebellion, since my Name is in him."

" If you listen carefully to what he says and do all that I say, I will be an enemy to your enemies and will oppose those who oppose you."

"My angel will go ahead of you and bring you into the land of the Amorites, Hittites, Perizzites, Canaanites, Hivites and Jebusites, and I will wipe them out."

" Do not bow down before their gods or worship them or follow their practices. You must demolish them and break their sacred stones to pieces."

"Worship the LORD your God and his blessing will be on your food and water. I will take away sickness from among you,

"and none will miscarry or be barren in your land. I will give you a full life span."

"I will send my terror ahead of you and throw into confusion every nation you encounter. I will make all your enemies turn their backs and run.

"I will send the hornet ahead of you to drive the Hivites, Canaanites and Hittites out of your way."

"But I will not drive them out in a single year, because the land would become desolate and the wild animals too numerous for you.

"Little by little I will drive them out before you, until you have increased enough to take possession of the land."

"I will establish your borders from the Red Sea to the Mediterranean Sea, and from the desert to the Euphrates River. I will give into your hands the people who live in the land, and you will drive them out before you.

"Do not make a covenant with them or with their gods.

"Do not let them live in your land or they will cause you to sin against me, because the worship of their gods will certainly be a snare to you."

Chapter Five

Genesis 2:15: "The Lord God took the man and put him in the Garden of Eden to work it and take care of it."

Genesis 1:26: "Then God said, 'Let us make mankind in our image, in our likeness, so that they may rule over the fish in the sea and the birds in the sky, over the livestock and all the wild animals, and over all the creatures that move along the ground.'"

Luke 19:17: "'Well done, my good servant!' his master replied. 'Because you have been trustworthy in a very small matter, take charge of ten cities.'"

Chapter Six

Mark 12:30-31: "'Love the Lord your God with all your heart and with all your soul and with all your mind and with all your strength.' The second is this: 'Love your neighbor as yourself.' There is no commandment greater than these."

Matthew 18:19-20: "Again, truly I tell you that if two of you on earth agree about anything they ask for, it will be done for them by my Father in heaven. For where two or three gather in my name, there am I with them."

John 14:30: "I will not say much more to you, for the prince of this world is coming. He has no hold over me."

Colossians 1:27: "To them God has chosen to make known among the Gentiles the glorious riches of this mystery, which is Christ in you, the hope of glory."

Chapter Seven

Exodus 23:27-28: "I will send my terror ahead of you and throw into confusion every nation you encounter. I will make all your enemies turn their backs and run. I will send the hornet ahead of you to drive the Hivites, Canaanites and Hittites out of your way."

Ephesians 6:12, NKJV: "For we do not wrestle against flesh and blood, but against principalities, against powers, against the rulers of the darkness of this age, against spiritual hosts of wickedness in the heavenly places."

Joshua 3:5: "Consecrate yourselves for tomorrow the Lord will do amazing things among you."

Chapter Eight

Acts 1:8: "But you will receive power when the Holy Spirit comes on you; and you will be my witnesses in Jerusalem, and in all Judea and Samaria, and to the ends of the earth."

Genesis 13:14-17: "The LORD said to Abram after Lot had parted from him, "Look around from where you are, to the north and south, to the east and west. All the land that you see I will give to you and your offspring forever. I will make your offspring like the dust of the earth, so that if anyone could count the dust, then your offspring could be counted. Go, walk through the length and breadth of the land, for I am giving it to you."

Joshua 6:16: "The seventh time around, when the priests sounded the trumpet blast, Joshua commanded the army, "Shout! For the LORD has given you the city!"

Joshua 6:20: "When the trumpets sounded, the army shouted, and at the sound of the trumpet, when the men gave a loud shout, the wall collapsed; so everyone charged straight in, and they took the city."

Exodus 34:12-14: "Be careful not to make a treaty with those who live in the land where you are going, or they will be a snare among you. Break down their altars, smash their sacred stones and cut down their Asherah poles. Do not worship any other god, for the LORD, whose name is Jealous, is a jealous God."

Luke 11:24-26, NKJV: "When an unclean spirit goes out of a man, he goes through dry places, seeking rest; and finding none, he says, 'I will return to my house from which I came.' And when he comes, he finds it swept and put in order. Then he goes and takes with him seven other spirits more wicked than himself, and they enter and dwell there; and the last state of that man is worse than the first."

Luke 6:28: "Bless those who curse you, pray for those who mistreat you."

Mark3:27: "In fact, no one can enter a strong man's house without first tying him up. Then he can plunder the strong man's house."

Chapter Nine

II Corinthians 10:4: "The weapons we fight with are not the weapons of the world. On the contrary, they have divine power to demolish strongholds."

Job 41:34: "It looks down on all that are haughty; it is king over all that are proud."

Job 42:3-6: "You asked, 'Who is this that obscures my plans without knowledge?' Surely I spoke of things I did not understand, things too wonderful for me to know. You said, 'Listen now, and I will speak; I will question you, and you shall answer me.' My ears had heard of you but now my eyes have seen you. Therefore I despise myself and repent in dust and ashes."

Isaiah 27:1: "In that day, the LORD will punish with his sword—his fierce, great and powerful sword—Leviathan the gliding serpent, Leviathan the coiling serpent; he will slay the monster of the sea."

I Samuel 14:7: "Do all that you have in mind," his armor-bearer said. "Go ahead; I am with you heart and soul" (verses 12-14), "The men of the outpost shouted to Jonathan and his armor-bearer, "Come up to us and we'll teach you a lesson." So Jonathan said to his armor-bearer, "Climb up after me; the LORD has given them into the hand of Israel." Jonathan climbed up, using his hands and feet, with his armor-bearer right behind him. The Philistines fell before Jonathan, and his armor-bearer followed and killed behind him. In that first attack Jonathan and his armor-bearer killed some twenty men in an area of about half an acre."

Chapter Ten

Ecclesiastes 3:1: "There is a time for everything, and a season for every activity under the heavens."

Mark 1:35: "Very early in the morning, while it was still dark, Jesus got up, left the house and went off to a solitary place, where he prayed."

I John 4:7-8: "Dear friends, let us love one another, for love comes from God. Everyone who loves has been born of God and knows God. Whoever does not love does not know God, because God is love."

II Corinthians 10:4: "The weapons we fight with are not the weapons of the world. On the contrary, they have divine power to demolish strongholds."

Ephesians 6:18: "And pray in the Spirit on all occasions with all kinds of prayers and requests. With this in mind, be alert and always keep on praying for all the Lord's people."

Matthew 7:22-23, NKJV: "Many will say to Me in that day, 'Lord, Lord, have we not prophesied in Your name, cast out demons in Your name, and done many wonders in Your name?' And then I will declare to them, 'I never knew you; depart from Me, you who practice lawlessness!'"

Ephesians 1:6, NKJV: "to the praise of the glory of His grace, by which He made us accepted in the Beloved."

Exodus 23:30: "Little by little I will drive them out before you, until you have increased enough to take possession of the land."

Ephesians 4:11: "So Christ himself gave the apostles, the prophets, the evangelists, the pastors and teachers."

James 3:1: "Not many of you should become teachers, my fellow believers, because you know that we who teach will be judged more strictly." (Verse 10): "Out of the same mouth come praise and cursing. My brothers and sisters, this should not be."

I Corinthians 13: "If I speak in the tongues of

men or of angels, but do not have love, I am only a resounding gong or a clanging cymbal. If I have the gift of prophecy and can fathom all mysteries and all knowledge, and if I have a faith that can move mountains, but do not have love, I am nothing. If I give all I possess to the poor and give over my body to hardship that I may boast, but do not have love, I gain nothing. Love is patient, love is kind. It does not envy, it does not boast, it is not proud. It does not dishonor others, it is not self-seeking, it is not easily angered, it keeps no record of wrongs. Love does not delight in evil but rejoices with the truth. It always protects, always trusts, always hopes, always perseveres.Love never fails. But where there are prophecies, they will cease; where there are tongues, they will be stilled; where there is knowledge, it will pass away. For we know in part and we prophesy in part, but when completeness comes, what is in part disappears. When I was a child, I talked like a child, I thought like a child, I reasoned like a child. When I became a man, I put the ways of childhood behind me. For now we see only a reflection as in a mirror; then we shall see face to face. Now I know in part; then I shall know fully, even as I am fully known.And now these three remain: faith, hope and love. But the greatest of these is love."

Jeremiah 9:23-24, NKJV: "let not the wise man glory in his wisdom, let not the might man glory in his strength, let not the rich man glory in his riches, let him that glories, glory in this: that he understands and knows God that he is the one that exercises loving kindness, justice and righteousness in all the earth for in these things he delights."

Ecclesiastes 12:13-14: "here is the conclusion of the matter, fear God, keep his commands for this is the whole duty of man."

Micah 6:8: "He has shown you, O mortal, what is good. And what does the Lord require of you? To act justly and to love mercy and to walk humbly with your God."

Psalm 1:1-3: "Blessed is the one who does not walk in step with the wicked or stand in the way that sinners take or sit in the company of mockers, but whose delight is in the law of the Lord, and who meditates on his law day and night. That person is like a tree planted by streams of water, which yields its fruit in season and whose leaf does not wither—whatever they do prospers."

Matthew 22:37-40: "Jesus replied: 'Love the Lord your God with all your heart and with all your soul and with all your mind.' This is the first and greatest commandment. And the second is like it: 'Love your neighbor as yourself.' All the Law and the Prophets hang on these two commandments."

James 4:2-3: "You do not have because you do not ask God. When you ask, you do not receive, because you ask with wrong motives, that you may spend it on what you get on your pleasures."

James 5:16-18: "The prayer of a righteous person is powerful and effective. Elijah was a human being, even as we are. He prayed earnestly that it would not rain, and it did not rain on the land for three and a half years. Again he prayed, and the heavens gave rain, and the earth produced its crops."

Luke 10:27: "He answered, 'Love the Lord your God with all your heart and with all your soul and with all your strength and with all your mind' and, 'Love your neighbor as yourself.'"

Esther 4:14: "For if you remain silent at this time, relief and deliverance for the Jews (all of the Lord's people!) will arise from another place, but you and your father's family will perish. And who knows but that you have come to your royal position for such a time as this?"

Recommended Reading

Final Quest Trilogy
Rick Joyner

Epic Battles of the Last Days
Rick Joyner

The Three Battlegrounds
Francis Frangipane

Holiness, Truth and the Presence of God
Francis Frangipane

Possessing the Gates of the Enemy
Cindy Jacobs

Authority in Prayer
Dutch Sheets

Releasing the Prophetic Destiny of a Nation
Dutch Sheets and Chuck Pierce

Time to Defeat the Devil
Chuck D. Pierce

Needless Casualties of War
John Paul Jackson

The Happy Intercessor
Beni Johnson

Set a Watch
Drs. Mahesh and Bonnie Chavda

Becoming a Prayer Warrior
Elizabeth Alves

Taking Our Cities for God
John Dawson

Engaging the Enemy
C. Peter Wagner

The Rules of Engagement
Cindy Trimm

Prayer Evangelism
Ed Silvoso

Never Surrender
Jerry Boykin

The Chronicles of Narnia
C. S. Lewis

The Screwtape Letters
C.S. Lewis

This Present Darkness
Frank E. Peretti